Wild, Wild World of Animals

Island Life

A TIME-LIFE TELEVISION BOOK

Editor: Eleanor Graves
Series Editor: Charles Osborne
Text Editor: Richard Oulahan
    Associate Text Editor: Bonnie Johnson
    Author: Marion Steinmann
    Writers: Deborah Heineman, Cecilia Waters
    Literary Research: Ellen Schachter
    Text Research: Mary Jane Hodges
    Copy Editors: Gregory Weed, Robert Braine
Picture Editor: Richard O. Pollard
    Picture Research: Judith Greene
    Permissions and Production: Cecilia Waters
Designer: Constance A. Timm
    Art Assistant: Carl Van Brunt
Production Editor: Joan Chambers

WILL, WILD WORLD OF ANIMALS

WILD, WILD WORLD OF ANIMALS
TELEVISION PROGRAM
Producers: Jonathan Donald and Lothar Wolff
This Time-Life Television Book is published by Time-Life Films, Inc.
Bruce L. Paisner, *President*
J. Nicoll Durrie, *Business Manager*

THE AUTHOR

MARION STEINMANN, a former science writer and associate editor of *Life*, is a free-lance journalist based in New York. Her articles have appeared in *The New York Times Magazine, Today's Health, Family Health, The Saturday Evening Post* and such other periodicals as the Time-Life *Nature/Science Annual*. A Cornell graduate, she is a holder of the American Medical Association's Medical Journalism Award.

THE CONSULTANTS

ROGER F. PASQUIER is the author of *Watching Birds: An Introduction to Ornithology*. He has worked as a curatorial assistant in the Department of Ornithology at the American Museum of Natural History in New York.

DR. RICHARD G. ZWEIFEL is Chairman and Curator in the Department of Herpetology of the American Museum of Natural History in New York. His fields of study include the ecology and systematics of reptiles and amphibians, in particular those of America and New Guinea. Dr. Zweifel has published more than 70 scientific papers in addition to semipopular articles for magazines and encyclopedias.

SIDNEY HORENSTEIN is on the staff of the Department of Invertebrates at the American Museum of Natural History, New York, and the Department of Geology and Geography, Hunter College. He has written many articles on natural history and has been a consultant on numerous Time-Life books. He publishes *New York City Notes on Natural History* and is Associate Editor of *Fossils Magazine*.

Wild, Wild World of Animals

Island Life

Based on the television series
Wild, Wild World of Animals

Published by
TIME-LIFE FILMS

The excerpt from Bridge to the Past by David Attenborough, copyright © 1961 by David Attenborough, is reprinted by permission of Lutterworth Press.

The excerpt from In Search of the Red Ape by John MacKinnon, copyright © 1974 by John MacKinnon, is reprinted by permission of Holt, Rinehart and Winston and William Collins, Ltd.

ISBN 0-913948-19-5

Library of Congress Catalog Card Number: 77-95115

Printed in the United States of America.

Contents

Introduction
by Marion Steinmann

THE MYRIAD ISLANDS, numerous beyond counting, that embellish the seas of this planet are as intriguing to connoisseurs of animal life as they are to vacationers seeking escape—and for some of the same reasons. For human beings there is something romantic and intrinsically satisfying about the very idea of an island—discrete, clearly defined, readily encompassed by the mind, free from the pressures of civilization. For man's fellow animals, too, the isolation of remote islands offers an easier existence. Because of their very insularity, islands are showcases of evolution, living laboratories where nature runs extraordinary experiments, nurturing and preserving novel animal species, encouraging eccentrics that on continents would be edged out or eaten up. The story of island creatures is the story of evolution itself.

Indeed, the peculiarities of island animals are so striking that they were among the seminal influences on the 19th century naturalist Charles Darwin and his discovery of the fact that animal species do evolve, over time, by the process he defined as natural selection—the survival of the species that are most successful at adapting to their environments.

Before Darwin, scientists generally accepted the premise, based on the Bible, that each animal species had been created independently in the place where it lived and that each was perfectly fitted from the beginning for the special environmental conditions of that place. The nature of each species was thought to be fixed and immutable. Darwin's faith in these notions was shaken when, during the 1830s, he sailed as ship's naturalist aboard a British Navy survey vessel, the *H.M.S. Beagle,* on a five-year, around-the-world expedition. As the ship visited the Cape Verde Islands in the Atlantic, South America, the Galápagos Islands in the Pacific, the South Sea Islands, New Zealand, Australia and the Indian Ocean, Darwin had ample opportunity to observe how animal populations vary in different parts of the globe. Darwin spent five weeks of the autumn of 1835 in the Galápagos, where he was struck by the remarkable resemblance of the flora and fauna he found to those of South America.

In the Galápagos, Darwin later wrote in *The Origin of Species,* "almost every product of the land and of the water bears the unmistakable stamp of the American continent. . . . The naturalist, looking at the inhabitants of these volcanic islands in the Pacific, distant several hundred miles from the continent, feels that he is standing on American land. Why should this be so? Why should the species which are supposed to have been created in the Galápagos Archipelago, and nowhere else, bear so plainly the stamp of affinity to those created in America? There is nothing in the conditions of life, in the geological nature of the islands, in their height or climate, or in the proportions in which the several classes are associated together, which closely resembles the conditions of the South American coast: in fact, there is a considerable dissimilarity in all these respects.

"On the other hand there is a considerable degree of resemblance in the volcanic nature of the soil, in the climate, height, and size of the islands, between the Galápagos and Cape Verde Archipelagoes: but what an entire and absolute difference in their inhabitants! The inhabitants of the Cape Verde Islands are related to those of Africa, like those of the Galápagos to America. Facts such as these admit of no sort of explanation on the ordinary view of independent creation."

Darwin and his fellow 19th century naturalist Alfred Russel Wallace divided the world's islands into two categories—"oceanic" islands and "continental" islands—on the basis of both their geologic origin and their flora and fauna. Oceanic islands, Wallace explained in his book, *Island Life*, "have originated in the ocean and have never formed part of a continent or any large mass of land [and are] usually far from continents and always separated from them by very deep sea." Continental islands, on the other hand, have "been separated from continents of which they are but detached fragments [and] are always more varied in their geological formation, containing both ancient and recent stratified rocks." Each geological type, Darwin and Wallace believed, had its own characteristic type of wildlife.

Modern geologists know that islands actually originate in many different ways from those known to Darwin and Wallace. In recent years, scientists have discovered that the earth's relatively brittle outer crust is broken up into a dozen or so colossal, rigid plates or slabs of rock, each about 40 miles thick, that float upon a denser, hotter and more mobile subterranean layer. It is the slow, ponderous movements of these so-called tectonic plates on their unstable foundations—their pulling apart and pushing together—that shape the earth's mountains and abysses, continents and islands.

More than 200 million years ago, the plates bearing the continents were all jammed together into a single enormous supercontinent that has been named Pangea, which in turn was divided into two halves: the southern part called Gondwanaland and the northern, Laurasia. As the ancient supercontinent split to form the present continents, islands were born, such as Madagascar. Some linear chains of volcanic islands—Hawaii for one—were built up as an oceanic plate moved over a relatively stationary "hot spot" in the deep underlying layer. Other volcanic islands have formed along the great submarine rifts in the ocean floors where plates are pulling apart and releasing molten lava from down below: The islands of St. Helena and Tristan da Cunha in the south Atlantic, for example, have arisen out of the mid-Atlantic rift that runs the entire length of that ocean. Still other kinds of islands have emerged where one ocean plate is colliding with another, casting up earth and volcanic deposits.

Many of the world's existing islands date back only to the end of the recent Ice Ages. At the height of the glaciation, so much of the planet's water supply was converted into ice that the world's sea level was some 375 feet lower than it is today. As the glaciers melted, the sea level gradually rose. The rising waters flooded low-lying parts of continents and carved out islands that are truly continental in the sense that they are

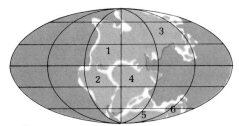

Pangea

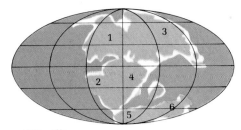

200 million years ago

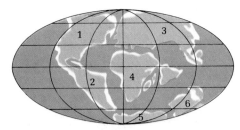

60 million years ago

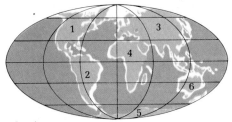

Ice Ages

1. North America
2. South America
3. Asia
4. Africa
5. Antarctica
6. Australia

Key to the formation of many islands is the process of continental drift and development shown above. Massive tectonic plates which formed part of the ancient supercontinent of Pangea broke apart over millions of years. Forces generated by this movement broke off such islands as Madagascar from continental rims and uplifted others, like Japan, along the edges of the plates.

This color engraving from a 19th century German natural history book shows a fanciful gathering of several species of Indonesian birds and mammals.

part of a continental shelf. Such was the origin of the British Isles, Ceylon, Taiwan, Tasmania and of some of the islands along the east coast of North America, such as Manhattan and Newfoundland. Another natural phenomenon has created some of the most enchanting islands of all: the many tropical atolls, with an oval ring of islands around a central lagoon, are built upon the eroded remnants of volcanoes by living colonies of coral.

Zoologically, perhaps one of the important factors in determining an island's animal life is whether or not it was connected by a land bridge during the last Ice Age, and the extent of glaciation. If afforded a land bridge, animals would simply have been able to circulate freely, from the continent to what is now the island and back again. Islands of this sort are said to have a continental fauna. The more recently such an island was cut off from its mainland, the less difference there is between its fauna and the mother continent. Great Britain, for instance, was connected to the Eurasian continent off and on until only about 7,000 years ago, when the rising sea level finally flooded the shallow English Channel. Consequently, its animals are all closely related to those of Western

Europe. If an island has never had a continental connection, it can only have acquired its terrestrial animals over the water by a process biologists call long-distance dispersal. Such islands can be said to have oceanic fauna.

How does long-distance dispersal come about? Some small animals reach even the most remote islands by raft. There is a considerable amount of debris drifting about in the sea at any time, including large, uprooted trees, with soil and stones still attached, and high-riding branches that could support an animal above the waves. In some parts of the world sizable floating islands are not uncommon, clumps of vegetation and soil held together by tangled roots, sometimes bearing trees 20 or 30 feet tall, all swept out to sea by some torrential flood.

Propelled by ocean currents, such rafts can readily carry insects and other invertebrates many hundreds of miles. Yet salt water is virtually an impassable barrier to many animal groups. Those least tolerant of salt water—and the least likely to be found on islands—are freshwater fish. The presence of strictly freshwater fish is, in itself, strong evidence that an island was fairly recently attached to a continent. The second group

Although the artist who made this early 19th century engraving entitled it "The Slow Maki," referring to a species of lemurs of Madagascar, the two tailless, wide-eyed creatures he depicted more closely resemble the lorises of Indonesia.

most vulnerable to salt water is the terrestrial mammals, particularly the larger ones, which generally do not have the endurance for long-distance swims and are unable to withstand long periods without fresh drinking water. Among land mammals, rodents are the hardiest voyagers and are often early arrivals on islands. Lizards, which are resistant to the desiccation brought about by exposure to salt water and which need little fresh drinking water, seem to be particularly good at traveling across oceans and are disproportionately numerous on many remote oceanic islands. Other animals arrive by air. Many migratory and water birds, of course, habitually fly distances over water, and it is no surprise to find them on the most distant islands, but even nonmigratory land birds frequently wander or are blown out to islands by storms. Bats, too, are almost always found on islands. Other, tinier animals are inadvertent stowaways; insects or snail eggs, for instance, can travel on a bird, stuck to its feathers or to its feet. Winds also waft light insects across long distances.

Obviously, there is an enormous element of hazard involved in long-distance dispersal. Of all the many animals that find themselves accidentally stuck to a bird or drifting out to sea on a log, very few will arrive alive on any island. There is a large element of chance, too, in whether such immigrants will find conditions for survival on an island. Herbivorous animals obviously cannot survive unless they find plants they can eat, and carnivorous animals cannot eat until the herbivores have settled in. For any species to reproduce and establish an island colony, two immigrants, a male and a female, or at the minimum a pregnant female, are needed. Uncrowded ecological niches must also be available for the new arrivals.

The weight of the odds would seem to be against such a series of events, but they nevertheless explain the gradual buildup of the present animal populations of faraway oceanic islands such as Hawaii, the Galápagos and New Zealand. The events need not necessarily be frequent: zoologist Elwood C. Zimmerman has calculated that for Hawaii only one successful immigration every 300,000 years would account for the island's present population of 70-odd species of land birds.

In this engraving, sailors, from a late
16th-century Dutch expedition, picnic on
the Indian Ocean island of Mauritius. One
giant tortoise provides a ponylike ride for
two men while the scooped-out shell of
another accommodates 10 others.

Two ground finches of the Galapagos Islands were painted by John Gould, an artist who worked from the specimens brought back by Charles Darwin from his round-the-world voyage on H.M.S. Beagle.

A modern case history of the hit-or-miss method of populating islands was the dramatic explosion and repopulation of Krakatoa, a small, volcanic island in Sunda Strait, between the islands of Sumatra and Java in the Indonesian archipelago. In 1883, the main Krakatoa volcano exploded catastrophically, with a roar heard as far away as Australia and Ceylon (present-day Sri Lanka), spewing ash 17 miles into the stratosphere and triggering seismic waves that killed 36,000 people on the coasts of Java and Sumatra. The explosion destroyed virtually all plant and animal life on Krakatoa. Yet a scientific survey made in 1908, only 25 years after the eruption, found the island already covered once again with vegetation, and botanists counted 115 different plant species. Thirteen nonmigratory land birds were found on Krakatoa in addition to 192 insect species, plus spiders, scorpions, snails and two kinds of lizards.

Another survey in 1933, 50 years after the disaster, found Krakatoa largely reforested, with some 270 plant species and 1,100 animal species. While Krakatoa is fairly close to Java (about 25 miles) and "the time since 1883 is short compared with geological times involved in population of most islands," explains botanist Sherwin Carlquist, the resurgence of Krakatoa's flora and fauna "is much like an accelerated version of what has happened on distant islands." When an immigrant species arrives in an island environment, it may evolve almost explosively. The relatively unfettered formation of new genetic strains on islands creates higher proportions of "endemic" species than on continents—that is, unique species found nowhere else on earth. The Hawaiian Islands have the highest percentage of endemic species of any place in the world: 95 percent of all the native plant and animal species are found only there.

Islands also acquire endemic species by preserving creatures that have evolved elsewhere but have become extinct everywhere else. Such animals are called relicts and are true living fossils, saved from extinction in an enisled museum. As islands foster endemic creatures, they tend to promote some characteristic oddities. One is extremity of size. Both the largest and the smallest lizards are island species. The largest known birds were two flightless islanders, now both extinct: the giant moa of New Zealand, one of which stood 12 feet tall, and Madagascar's elephant bird, *Aepyornis*, which was the heaviest bird ever known. *Aepyornis* weighed up to half a ton, stood 10 feet tall, laid a two-gallon egg and may have inspired the *Arabian Nights* legend of the roc, an Indian Ocean bird that carried off elephants to feed its young.

Perhaps the oddest bodily change produced on islands is the loss among birds and insects of the ability to fly. While aeronautical skill obviously helps get an animal to an island safely in the first place, once there the animal often tends to settle down and abandon flight altogether, because the island environment is less dangerous and difficult than the habitat where the creature originated.

The most poignant consequence of the freer and easier island life is that in permitting the survival of so many less-adaptable creatures, islands thus harbor animals so vulnerable that they are unable to compete when their cloistered environment changes. The story of island creatures is also the story of extinction. As man has invaded islands, introduced domestic animals and formerly absent predators, felled the forests and hunted the native animals, the fragile islanders have in too many cases vanished. Indeed, the very symbol of extinction is a former island dweller: the dodo, an improbable-looking, flightless bird that lived on the Indian Ocean island of Mauritius and managed to survive only 173 years after Europeans first explored the island in 1507.

Madagascar

Rising out of the Indian Ocean just 250 miles off the southeast coast of Africa, the massive island of Madagascar is clearly a geographical satellite of that continent, and indeed it was once physically joined to Africa, with its western bulge tucked neatly into a bay of the present coast of Mozambique and Tanzania. Both Madagascar and Africa were at that time part of an ancient Southern Hemisphere supercontinent called Gondwanaland, which also encompassed Antarctica, India, Australia and South America. Gondwanaland began to break up 200 million years ago. Later, Madagascar was one of the first islands to be cast off and it slowly drifted seaward to its present location.

Sprawling nearly 1,000 miles from north to south and with an area of 228,000 square miles, Madagascar—known briefly as the Malagasy Republic—is the fourth-largest island in the world and has an almost continental range of climates and habitats. A spine of high plateaus and mountains, with peaks that thrust upward to nearly 9,500 feet, runs the length of the island, so that while temperatures may be hot on the coasts, they are often cool in the highlands. The southeasterly trade winds that sweep across the Indian Ocean are intercepted by the mountain backbone, dumping copious rain on the eastern side of the island and leaving the southwest side an arid semidesert.

With such variegated climate and topography, and with the proximity of Africa, the flora and fauna of Madagascar ought to look very much like those of the great continent. Yet biologically Madagascar is not African at all. Most of its human population came across the water from the east, from the Indonesian region. Much of its plant life is related to that of New Caledonia and other southwestern Pacific Ocean islands. And its wildlife is totally different from that of Africa. Madagascar has none of the large, dramatic African animals—no elephants or lions, no great herds of wildebeests. Instead, Madagascar has its own remarkable mix of wild creatures, some of them found no place else on earth and all small scale, with the largest measuring no more than three feet.

The big island's greatest claims to faunal fame are the lemurs, appealing, monkeylike forest dwellers with wet noses, grasping hands and feet, and large, staring eyes that give them a ghostly appearance and account for their name—from the Latin *lemures*, meaning phantoms of the dead. Lemurs are among the most primitive of the primates, and they live only in Madagascar.

Of the three families and 21 species of Madagascar lemuroids, only six species can properly be called lemurs. These are the so-called "true" lemurs. The commonest of them is the gregarious ringtail, which has a clownish face and a black-and-white striped tail like a raccoon. The second family (Indridae) of four genera includes the three-foot indris (Malagasy for "There it is!"), the largest survivor of their now extinct, and legendary, ancestors, which were the size of little men. The smallest of the indrisoids is the woolly avahi, a furry but unfriendly nocturnal animal. The handsomest members are the two sifakas, one a dark-furred resident of the moist tropical zones and the other a white-furred beauty with a dusky face (opposite), which prefers a cool, dry habitat.

The third family has a single and singular member, the solitary and nocturnal aye-aye, which was long considered to be a squirrel because of its rodentlike teeth. The aye-aye is not only odd, it is also one of the world's rarest creatures. With much of their forest habitat destroyed, virtually all of the Madagascar lemurs are now endangered, none more so than the aye-aye, with only a few individuals remaining in the wild and 11 on a special island reserve.

Besides the lemurs, Madagascar has a collection of other quaint and curious animals, including such unique species as the tenrecs, prickly, primitive insectivores that look somewhat like a children's book drawing of a hedgehog, half the world's species of chameleons, and iguanas whose closest living relative is 6,000 miles away in South America. The almost 70 species of mammals include the cosmopolitan bats and rats, which occur on almost all islands, and just 11 carnivores, all viverrids (civets, genets and mongooses), the largest of which is the catlike fossa.

Scientists are just as perplexed by the animals that are not on Madagascar as they are by the indigenous creatures themselves. There are 150-odd species of frogs but no toads or other amphibians. No poisonous snakes exist on the big island, and there are no freshwater fish in its streams. Madagascar's 82 species of birds (well over half of them endemic) are nothing to compare with the rich avian population of neighboring Africa. The island's fauna is so unbalanced, in fact, that it suggests that all of Madagascar's animal life may have gotten there by flying, rafting or swimming across salt water.

One outlander that definitely reached the island from overseas was man, and from the ecological point of view he

was the most undesirable of all aliens. When people came to Madagascar from out of the East some 2,000 years ago, they discovered a land covered with humid tropical rain forests, drier, more temperate deciduous woodlands, open savannas and, in the extreme south, scrubland with cactus-like vegetation. Since then the two-legged invaders have cut down so much of the forest and denuded so much of the land that vast areas of the island's reddish soil are now exposed, leading to the nickname the Big Red Island. With the destruction of the land and the animal habitats, the wildlife of Madagascar has suffered an appalling parallel decline. So many species have been extirpated and so many others are on the brink of extinction that, despite belated efforts at conservation, the Big Red Island may one day become the Big Dead Island.

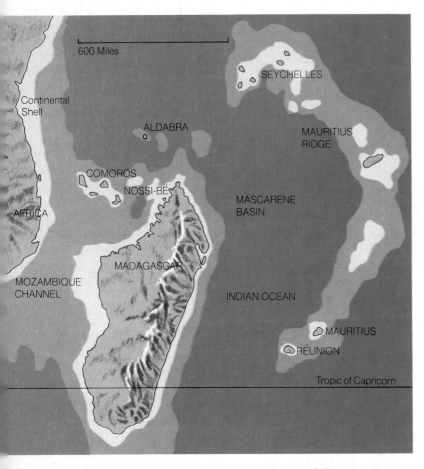

Second-growth trees dot grassland near Bekily in southern Madagascar. Lighter shades of blue in the map (and in similar maps on following pages) indicate shallower water. The lightest shade marks the continental shelves of Africa and the island, which were once attached to each other.

18

A young ring-tailed lemur peeks over its mother's shoulder (left) as she and another troop member forage for leaves. Fruits make up the major part of the lemur's diet, and cultivated banana groves are frequent targets for poaching. The lemurs' noisy quarrels over the fruit usually alert the planters to their presence.

A small group of ringtails (right) huddles together while they engage in mutual grooming, a favorite pastime. The baby lemur holds onto its mother in a position parallel to her body. Such behavior is typical of the higher primates but not of most lemurs. The young of all the other lemur species lie horizontally across their mother's belly.

Lemur Society

Lemurs make up approximately two-fifths of all the mammals found in Madagascar. Of the so-called true lemurs, the prototypical ring-tailed lemur, seen on these pages, is the most numerous. Although most lemurs are arboreal, inhabiting Madagascar's forested areas, the ringtail is more terrestrial and lives in rocky crevices in the island's arid, sparsely wooded regions. Like all lemurs, the ringtail is a sociable creature that lives in family groups or troops numbering between five and 20 animals. Although the majority of its members are males, the group is usually headed by one or more of the older females. Such an uneven sexual ratio and the competition it stirs among the males probably acts to stimulate courtship during the breeding season.

Following mating and after a gestation period of four and a half months, one, sometimes two, young are born between March and June. Born with a coat of short, thick fur and large, open eyes, the infant lemur generates great excitement among the troop members, who vie with one another for a chance to hold and lick it. The youngster is cared for by both its parents but it generally travels with its mother, clinging to her abdomen until it is about two weeks old, when it is strong enough to ride securely on her back as she leaps from tree to tree or runs agilely on the ground in search of food.

Ring-tailed lemurs, members of the same troop, lick each other's faces in greeting (below). To a stranger, such a greeting—though initially friendly—may suddenly turn hostile, lead to serious fighting and end with the intruder seeking membership in another troop.

A contented troop of ringtails, sun lovers like all lemurs, takes time out at right from the daily search for food to sit—arms and legs extended, bellies exposed—and soak up the warming rays.

The red ruffed lemur (left) is a separate color phase of the ruffed lemur (below). Like its relative, the red ruffed lemur is nocturnal, but small family groups of the graceful animals often gather together to bask in the morning sun.

The abundant fruit of the breadfruit tree is a dietary perquisite of the black lemur (opposite). Bananas, however, make up the major portion of its diet. Only the male of the species is black. The female's distinctively different brownish-red coloration once led scientists to believe she was a separate species.

The ruffed lemur (below) is the largest of all the true lemurs, measuring two feet long from its head to its rump. The bold black-and-white pattern of its fur serves as an effective camouflage in the sunlight and shadows of its forest habitat.

Rare Tree Dwellers

Five species of true lemurs live mainly in trees, and as a consequence, they have become increasingly rare with the clearing of Madagascar's forests. Among them are the three seen here. The handsome ruffed lemur (right), with its face-framing fringe of fur, is the only member of the family that builds a nest for its young. Unlike the fully furred newborn ringtails, ruffed lemur babies are born almost naked and remain in their nests for their first few weeks of life, where they are suckled by their mother each night.

The red ruffed lemur (above) rouses at dusk and leaps through branches in search of leaves and fruit. The black lemur (opposite) frequents the tallest trees of northwest Madagascar. Known for its swiftness, this generally vegetarian lemur sometimes preys on jungle birds, whose brains are among its favorite foods.

Simianesque Sifakas

The most monkeylike of the lemurs are the sifakas—members, along with the indris and the avahis, of the family Indridae. The indrids differ from the Lemuridae in having flattened muzzles and more elongated hands.

Sifakas are primarily arboreal, climbing through the trees with a slow, deliberate hand-over-hand motion. They frequently descend to the ground where they move around in an upright position with short, hopping jumps, arms raised for balance. More often, however, sifakas get from one tree to another by prodigious leaps. They are aided in this by a membrane, a flap of skin that extends from each arm to either side of the chest and functions as a kind of parachute. Once they have landed, they often sit with their hands on their knees, palms turned toward the sun. This posture has led to the Malagasy superstition that sifakas are an animal cult of sun worshipers.

A group of sifakas (above) feeds tranquilly on leaves. Sifakas hold onto branches with their long, narrow hands and powerful grasping legs. These hind limbs also help them gain footholds when they leap from tree to tree (top, right). Distances of 30 and 40 feet are easily spanned by these handsome animals. Although they are diurnal, sifakas generally rest in the branches of the forest trees (bottom, right) during the heat of the day, communicating with one another through clucking sounds that resemble the cackle of chickens.

Bridge to the Past

by David Attenborough

When David Attenborough, an English naturalist and photographer, went to Madagascar to study its unique animal life, he was well acquainted with the local legend of a dog-headed man. Attenborough's account of his observations, Bridge to the Past, *offers the following diary on the life of the indris, a rare lemur which may well be the prototype of the mythical creature.*

We came to recognize the family individually. The old male was of a phlegmatic disposition and somewhat sedate. He often sat on a branch with his back against the main trunk and his long legs outstretched in a comically human-like position. Although he could leap great distances when he was alarmed, he usually clambered from one branch to another. He never, however, used his arms in the way apes do—to swing from one bough to another—and as a trapeze artist, he could not compare with, say, a gibbon.

The two youngsters were an extremely affectionate couple and spent hours each day caressing and licking one another. The position they chose in which to practise their endearments, squatting on a thin horizontal bough, seemed very perilous. They reminded me of a pair of skilful circus acrobats nonchalantly pretending to enact the ordinary episodes of their daily lives on a high wire. But the indris had no need of balancing poles or safety nets. Their feet were so large that with their middle and big toes they could completely encircle the branch on which they sat with a grip so firm and steady that there was no need to cling on to anything with their hands. They were, however, rather skittish and nervous. Any sudden noise, whether made by us or by some other forest creature, alarmed them. A couple of black parrots flying overhead squawking raucously would make them crane their heads up anxiously. Once as they sat facing one another, the male

gently licking the fur of the female's neck, a large blue coua, the Madagascan cuckoo, came hopping up one of the lianas, grunting its loud gruff staccato call. The female immediately abandoned her relaxed posture and sat upright, twisting her head to try and identify the creature that produced this alarming noise. The male looked down too, less alarmed, and then made a tentative effort to resume his affectionate lickings. But the female remained tense and nervous, so the male reached up to a branch by his head and neatly swung himself round so that he sat behind his mate. Then he placed one of his long legs on either side of her, as though to reassure her. She bent back her long neck and rewarded him with a lick on the chin.

The fourth member of the family group, the old female, we seldom saw. She seemed to settle only in the thickest foliage. Perhaps she had good cause for her reticence. It was only after several days of concentrating our attention on her that we discovered the reason. Clinging to her back, she had a small black-faced baby with hairy puckish ears and bright eyes. He was barely a foot long. Sometimes he rode on her back, sometimes he clambered round to suckle from his mother's nipples. She behaved with endearing tenderness towards him, licking him gently from time to time.

Our detailed knowledge of the family's daily routine made our task of filming them much easier. We had photographed them feeding, dozing and caressing one

another, but one shot we lacked. We had never secured any good pictures of the indris leaping, for when they did finally move off, they always jumped away from us. If we were to get the film we wanted, then we should have to devise some new method of approach. We knew their lunch-time tree and we knew where they sang in the late afternoon. To get from one place to the other, we realized that they would have to cross a wide road leading from the fish ponds. At only one place was it narrow enough for the indris to leap comfortably from one side to the other. A simple calculation was enough to show that they must make the crossing between three and four o'clock in the afternoon. Accordingly at half-past two, Geoff and I set up our cameras a little west of the trees we judged they would use, so that the sun was behind our backs. We waited.

Prompt at half-past three, the old male appeared in the take-off tree. The young couple joined him a few minutes later, and finally the mother and her baby emerged from the forest behind to sit on one of the branches overhanging the road. As soon as they were all assembled, the old male clambered leisurely to the most outstretched branch. Geoff began filming. The male poised himself, then leaped, a single soaring jump right across the road to the tree on the other side. One by one, the rest of his family followed him and disappeared. Geoff switched off his cameras, beaming. Our film of the private life of the indris was at last as complete as we could have hoped to make it.

Holdouts

The rarest of the lemuroids are the avahi (right) and the aye-aye (below). Both are cat-sized creatures with bodies that measure about 17 inches long and tails of the same length or even longer. Avahis, members of the family In-dridae, lead predominantly arboreal lives, clinging verti-cally to the trunks or limbs of trees, where they feed on leaves, buds and bark. They are found only in eastern and northwestern Madagascar.

The aye-aye, an extremely endangered lemuroid species that numbers only an estimated 50 surviving individuals, is the lone member of the family Daubentoniidae. It has a number of rodentlike features, such as ever-growing, chisel-sharp incisors and clawlike nails on its hands and feet. The aye-aye's distinctive hands, with their slender, bony fingers and an exaggeratedly long third finger, are used for grooming as well as for digging out wood-boring insects and their larvae from under the bark of trees. The aye-aye's keen sense of hearing enables it to detect the movements of larvae in the wood. By tapping a tree with its elongated third finger it can also discern differences in timbre in the wood caused by the presence of larvae.

Large eyes are a typical feature of such nocturnal animals as the alert aye-aye above and the huddled trio of wide-eyed avahis at right. These lemuroids spend the daylight hours sleeping in tree hollows and move sluggishly if disturbed during that time. At night, however, when they are foraging for food, they are extremely active and lively.

Persistent Tenrecs

One of the most primitive mammals, with ancestors dating from the Pleistocene epoch one million years ago, the Malagasy tenrec is an adaptable animal, related to the hedgehog, that has proved itself a successful survivor. Some of the 30 species have evolved long prehensile tails, others have webbed feet for semiaquatic habitats, and some, called "Madagascar hedgehogs," have developed thick, protective hedgehog-style spines. Tenrecs are insectivores, widely distributed throughout the forests, scrub grasslands and marshes of Madagascar.

Among the more highly developed species are the streaked tenrecs, which dig burrows that can be inhabited by as many as 22 individuals living together amicably.

Large litters of up to 11 and rapid growth are extra survival insurance for these prickly little creatures. The streaked tenrec feeds on invertebrates such as earthworms, sucking them up from the ground into its mouth. Streaked tenrecs hunt food in parties that are a study in group cooperation. When one animal spots food, it dances about, signaling to the others to search the nearby terrain by jiggling a special spiny area on its back. The resulting vibrations may produce sound signals that are inaudible to the human ear. On the hunt, streaked tenrecs resemble so many four-legged Charlie Chaplins—hind feet pointing out at right angles to their bodies as they scurry through the forest, searching for earthworms or other quarry.

Threatened, a Madagascar hedgehog (opposite) snarls, rolls itself into a ball and erects a formidable pincushion of white-tipped spines—an illusory but effective imitation of quivering size and strength. Any predator incautious enough to touch the thorny creature will receive a painful wound.

A streaked tenrec (right) raises its neck spines in a menacing ruff. When disturbed, it lowers and raises its head in a threatening manner. This subspecies is predominantly black with chestnut markings and a stripe from muzzle to ears.

A Madagascar hedgehog (below) pauses in its search for insects. Its limbs terminate in five clawed digits well adapted for digging.

When the sharp eyes of a fossa (left) sight an unwary bird or lemur, the animal takes off in pursuit of its quarry, which it catches with its razor-sharp retractable claws. The alert little fanaloka (below), with the spotted coat and slender limbs typical of its species, prowls the rain-forest floor in search of the small mammals that make up its diet.

Fossa and Fanaloka

The largest of Madagascar's 11 carnivores, the catlike fossa (opposite), and its close relative, the fanaloka (above), inhabit forested areas of the island. Once considered a true cat, the fossa has been reclassified as a separate subfamily of the viverrids. Shuffling peacefully through the forest, with its short legs and flat-footed walk, it seems unaware of the dwindling number of trees in its habitat, a result of the growth of populated areas and a serious threat to the survival of forest dwellers. The fossa's tendency to invade farmyards and prey on chickens has made it unpopular with the Malagasy natives who hunt and kill what they regard as a threat to their livelihood. Over the years, exaggerated tales of the fossa's viciousness and ferocity have given the animal an undeservedly notorious reputation.

The foxlike fanaloka is found in the Madagascan rain forest, near streams, where it can feed easily on semiaquatic tenrecs. Smaller than the fossa it is even more vulnerable and is becoming increasingly rare.

Lizards in Ambush

More than half the world's chameleons, including the largest and the smallest individual species, are natives of Madagascar. They and their close lizard kin, the island's 50 species of geckos, have very different techniques for stalking the insects they eat. The gecko pounces on its prey in a flash of aggressive speed. Its wide, flattened toes have microscopic adhesive structures that enable the little lizard to grasp the smoothest surfaces and to walk up a sheer vertical wall or even across a ceiling. The chameleon's hunting technique is to quietly creep up on its prey. Its protuding eyes, encased in cone-shaped lids, scan the vicinity independently of each other, and its tail and opposable toes are able to cling effortlessly to a leafy branch. When the chameleon encounters its insect prey, its tongue, longer than its body, darts out and the insect is captured on the sticky tip and zipped into the mouth of the motionless reptile in a fraction of a second—faster than the human eye is able to see.

Jaws gaping in anger, the leaf-tailed gecko (left) presents a sinister aspect. The pupils of its large eyes are closed to a slit in the bright sunlight. Its barklike brown skin provides an excellent disguise.

A chameleon (right) lies in ambush for an unsuspecting insect. The chameleon's celebrated ability to change color is due to the expansion or the contraction of pigment-containing cells, triggered by its mood as well as by temperature, light intensity and background coloration.

Glowing green coloration is perfect camouflage for the Madagascar day gecko (below). Most active during the bright daylight hours, it blends in with the foliage even when moving.

The Seychelles and Aldabra

After the caravels of Vasco da Gama pioneered a maritime route to the Orient in 1498, the Indian Ocean became one of the world's great sea lanes. The islands along the way were the recipients, willy-nilly, of all the dubious benefits of European colonization and commercial exploitation.

Each of the isolated islands and island groups was a sanctuary for unique and fragile forms of wildlife— flightless birds, specialized prosimians and carnivores, and one-of-a-kind amphibians. Each, with dismaying rapidity and thoroughness, was despoiled and its distinctive fauna exterminated by the white man and the dogs, hogs and other predators he brought with him. Today, two tiny mid-ocean island groups, the Seychelles and Aldabra, remain as sanctuaries for animals of the Indian Ocean area that can be found nowhere else on earth. The Seychelles, which were relatively late to feel the machete of the coconut planter and only recently became a vacation resort, are still the home of some remarkable and mysterious amphibians. Aldabra, with little potable water and almost no arable soil, remains the only unexploited group of islands left in the vast ocean, and the last bastion of its giant tortoises and its only remaining flightless birds.

The two groups are neighbors of Madagascar, closer to that enormous island than to any other large land mass— the Seychelles lie 657 miles northeast of Madagascar, and Aldabra 265 miles northwest. The wildlife of both island groups is closely related to that of Madagascar. Both the Seychelles and Aldabra are zoologically oceanic, with mainly those animal tenants that have drifted, swum or flown there across hundreds of miles of salt water. Both groups are also so small in area—the Seychelles no more than 156 square miles and Aldabra about 60 square miles—that neither can begin to offer animals the space or the diversity of climates and habitats that Madagascar can. Thus the Seychelles and Aldabra have no native land mammals at all, except for the omnipresent bats.

The Seychelles lie entirely within the tropics, five degrees south of the Equator, and consist of 92 islands and islets. The largest, Mahé, is about 55 square miles in area, with the groups' highest point of land, Morne Seychellois, which rises to 2,971 feet. The climate is unusually steady, with an average temperature of 79° F., and the rain falls in spates of 90 inches a year. Despite this favorable climate and the islands' scenic beauty, with emerald hills flowing down to palm-fringed beaches, the Seychelles were by-passed by man and remained uninhabited—and their wildlife undisturbed—until the late 18th century, when French settlers named them after a government official and established a colony there. Subsequently the Seychelles passed into the British Empire and their natural tropical forest was cleared for coconut plantations. Since 1976, they have been politically independent.

The Seychelles have fascinated naturalists since the time of Charles Darwin and Alfred Russel Wallace because they are a geological anomaly: Alone among mid-ocean islands, some of them are formed not of volcanic rock but of granite, a hard, crystalline rock that can be formed only under the conditions of intense pressure found in continents. Geologists today realize that the Seychelles, like Madagascar, must be fragments of Gondwanaland, the ancient Southern Hemisphere supercontinent that split up 200 million years ago. Over the years, the Seychelles have served as an evolutionary incubator for 15 known endemic species of birds, including the world's smallest true falcon, the Seychelles kestrel, which weighs only six ounces and is about the size of a European starling. There are a few local species of snakes and lizards, but it is in its collection of endemic amphibians that the Seychelles have acquired several real museum pieces. Three tiny frogs, belonging to an endemic family, Sooglossidae, are unlike any frogs living on any of the nearby land masses, Madagascar or Africa or India. The strangest Seychelles amphibian, however, is an endemic caecilian, Hypogeophis—and the strangest thing about it is that it is there at all. Caecilians are legless, wormlike burrowing creatures that, along with the anurans (frogs and toads) and urodeles (salamanders), form the three orders of amphibians. Of the three orders, the caecilians are the least adapted for crossing salt water. And there are no caecilians on nearby Madagascar. Yet unaccountably, they are on the Seychelles.

Though politically part of the Seychelles, Aldabra is geologically quite distinct; it is a low coral atoll of four main islands encircling a central lagoon. The largest, South Island, is about 20 miles long and rises only 20 to 30 feet above the sea. Since their formation, the islands have been cast up and then eroded by waves, so that in many places the land balloons out over the water line, overhanging the sea like giant mushrooms.

Aldabra has been the evolutionary incubator of 10 to 12 species of endemic land birds, including a white-throated

rail that is the only flightless bird left in the Indian Ocean, once the home of the dodo and other birds that lost the power of flight. The little atoll is most famous today as the last remaining abode of the Indian Ocean giant land tortoise, which can reach 400 pounds or more. Two hundred years ago, these colossal chelonians inhabited many other islands in the Indian Ocean, including both Madagascar and the Seychelles. Unfortunately, however, their flesh is savory and nourishing, they can survive long voyages aboard ship without food or water and one tortoise can feed a vessel's crew for days. As a result, they were hunted so relentlessly that by the early part of the 19th century they were exterminated almost everywhere but on Aldabra. Here, at least, they seem in little danger: A census in the late 1960s put the surviving population at about 80,000.

For all their formidable size, the giant tortoises are benign. One visitor, photographer Tony Beamish, author of *Aldabra Alone,* found himself growing fond of them. "They are perfect company if you like peace and quiet but not unbroken solitude," he commented. "They are friendly and call on you but never overstay their welcome. Their siesta time is the same as yours. Their slow movement and occasional noises, clattering carapace, the quiet hiss, a rare throaty roar, is comforting in a moon landscape that is often so silent you can hear the grass grow."

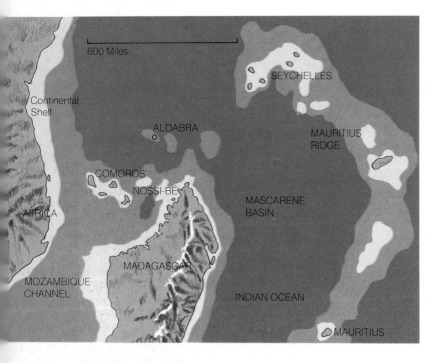

Tide ruffles the waters of an inlet on Mahé Island in the Seychelles. The beauty of these islands, now accessible through an international jetport, has made them a popular resort—further threatening the fragile existence of the local wildlife.

Island-Hoppers

Lizards are the most successful of reptile island-hoppers, appearing in great numbers on tropical and subtropical islands around the world. Among the islanders none are more ubiquitous than the geckos and skinks. The burnished bronze mabuya skinks (above and below) and the leaf-green Seychelles gecko, *Phelsuma abbotti* (opposite), are natives of the Seychelles.

The Seychelles gecko is a tree dweller and, unlike most other geckos, which are active at dusk and in the night, it is diurnal. It is one of 24 known species of day geckos—with skins in as many varying shades of green and often embellished with a sprinkling of red on their backs—that inhabit many of the Indian Ocean islands. Both the arboreal geckos and the ground-hugging mabuyas are primarily insectivores. But the mabuya will eat almost anything that moves and is not too big—even a mouse.

When the occasion presents itself, a mabuya skink will even consume a member of its own Scincidae family (left). The sinuous skinks are a family in transition: Some members have become legless.

A group of mabuyas waits hungrily for leftovers (left) while a fat relation feasts on a broken tern egg. Scientists speculate that skinks became islanders by riding on floating jetsam and natural rafts.

For maximum camouflage, the Seychelles day gecko (right) changes its hue from bright grass green to olive to dark green, depending on its surroundings. On Aldabra the tiny lizard lives symbiotically with the giant tortoises (overleaf).

The green day gecko on the shell of the Aldabra tortoise above is no chance visitor: The two very different reptiles share a fine symbiotic relationship. Living on the edges of a tortoise's carapace, geckos feed on the insects that are attracted by the big turtle's excretions. In turn, the overhanging edges of the carapace offer the tiny lizards a shady place for their midday siestas and a safe refuge where they sleep at night. The Aldabra tortoises are the largest land turtles in the world, weighing slightly more than their closest relatives, the giant tortoises of the Galápagos Islands (pages 78–79) that live halfway around the world.

Using the carapace of a companion for a lift up, a cumbersome Aldabran tortoise reaches for the sparse foliage of a local bush. Vegetarian and mild of nature, the Aldabrans have a keen and mysterious sense of time, awaking, eating, napping, sunning themselves and going to sleep at the same times each day. They may also hold the world's longevity record. Centenarians are commonplace, and there are reports of giant tortoises that have lived for 200 or more years.

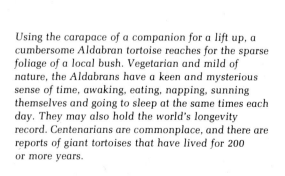

Redoubt of the Island Giants

When the early explorers first ventured into the Indian Ocean they were greeted by hordes of giant, lumbering land tortoises on almost every island where they landed. On some islands the amiable creatures were so numerous that they literally covered the landscape, carapace to carapace, to the local horizon. Unfortunately for the tortoises, they proved to be an appetizing and plentiful source of fresh meat: Taken aboard ship and dumped into the hold, the tortoises could survive for months on the long cruises of the sailing era without food or water.

The tortoise islands thus became regular victualing stops for ships of all kinds and, over a period of nearly three centuries, the great creatures disappeared from island after island: Most of them were exterminated altogether. Today, only a few specimens of the Seychelles giant tortoise survive in a zoo on Mahé. The only place where the creatures live on in the wild is Aldabra.

Happily, the future of the Aldabra tortoise seems secure. The danger of the shipboard stewpot vanished with the sailing ships, and the estimated 80,000 tortoises that survive on Aldabra are rigidly protected. They have nothing to fear from the humans who share the atoll with them: The natives regard them with affection and give them such regal names as "Queen Malila."

Fairies and Noddies

Like most oceanic islands, the Seychelles and Aldabra are home base for terns, which cover the local waterfronts and breed together in noisy, gregarious congregations. Graceful, long-winged water birds, the terns are masters of flight and expert divers underwater in pursuit of fish. But ashore they are usually awkward, handicapped by their weak legs and small feet.

Most terns are predominantly white with black caps, but the two specimens shown here are exceptions. The fairy tern (below) has no black cap, making it the only completely white member of the family, except for its black bill and black eye feathers. It also has a fanlike tail, unlike the characteristic forked tail of most terns. The lesser noddy (opposite) and the common noddy reverse the usual family color contrasts with feathers that are completely brown, except for an off-white head.

The fairy tern (left) dispenses completely with nests: The female lays a single egg in the fork of a tree, on a rock or even on a doorstep, and must then brood standing up, lest the egg be dislodged by sitting on it. The hatchling baby teeters on its perch for several days before it finally falls or jumps to the ground. Such haphazard incubators are so precarious and exposed—to predators like skinks and to the wind—that it seems miraculous that any eggs or hatchlings survive.

Lesser noddy terns (right), some brooding eggs in untidy nests, crowd the branches of a dead tree in the Seychelles. The slightly larger and lighter common noddy, a near relative, also inhabits the islands, and the two resemble each other so closely that sometimes the only way to distinguish them is by the location of their nests: Common noddies nest mostly on the ground, lesser noddies in the trees.

The West Indies

The curving arc of the West Indies outlines the Caribbean Sea with a 2,500-mile chain of islands and islets, forming a bulwark between the sparkling sea and the gray Atlantic Ocean and almost linking the North and South American continents. At the northern end are the Bahamas group, followed by the four Greater Antilles, the largest islands of the archipelago: Cuba, Jamaica, Hispaniola (politically divided into Haiti in the west and the Dominican Republic in the east) and Puerto Rico. Hooking southward and then westward again like a giant shepherd's crook in the sea, are the Lesser Antilles, their names reflecting the many languages of the buccaneers and the colonists who followed Columbus into this new world: the Virgin Islands, Guadeloupe, Dominica, Martinique, Saint Lucia, Tobago, Trinidad, Curaçao, Aruba and other islands in the sun. Almost entirely within the tropics, the Caribbean isles have an unvaryingly balmy climate—year-round temperatures average about 80° F. and seldom fall below 70° F., and the trade winds drop a bountiful 65 inches of rain a year.

Geologically and zoologically, the Caribbean islands divide into two distinct areas, with the island of Trinidad standing sharply apart from all the others. Geologically, Trinidad is part of a continent. It perches less than 10 miles off the coast of South America, at the mouth of Venezuela's Orinoco River, and was until recently connected with the continent by land bridges.

Zoologically, Trinidad is also an extension of the continent. For a relatively small island (1,864 square miles), Trinidad has a rich, well-balanced fauna, all of it essentially South American, with relatively few endemic species. It has the strictly freshwater fish that are a measure of the continental or oceanic character of an island. There are almost a dozen frogs and toads on Trinidad and a number of snakes, including some poisonous ones. The island skies swarm with brilliantly colored tropical birds: parrots, toucans, trogons, jacamars and, appropriately for what the calypso singers call "the land of the hummingbird," 16 species of the jewel-like little birds. The mammals of Trinidad are all related to South American forms: four opossums, two anteaters, an armadillo (which the Spanish named "little armed one" because of the horny plates protecting its body), a deer, the piglike collared peccary, the tayra (a relative of the weasel), the ocelot and two monkeys—the vivacious sapajou and the red howler, one of the largest of the New World simians, which pro-

claims its presence with a roar that can be heard for miles. Two species of true vampire bats are also found on Trinidad, where they suck the blood of cattle, goats and birds and have been known to attack sleeping humans.

The other islands of the West Indies have had a totally different geological origin from Trinidad. These islands were created 40 million years ago by the same sort of undersea collision between the earth's crustal plates that produced the Japanese archipelago, and, like Japan (page 114), they are an arcing island chain. The American plate, which carries half of the floor of the Atlantic and both of the American continents, is moving westward. Hundreds of miles of it have plunged beneath the Caribbean plate along the outlying Puerto Rico Trench, forming the greatest depth in the Atlantic, 28,374 feet. The northern boundary of the Caribbean plate runs along the Cayman Trench, a great canyon in the floor of the Caribbean Sea, which extends from southern Cuba to the Gulf of Honduras, and then is presumed to cross Central America along a fault line to meet the easterly moving Cocos plate in the Pacific. Thus, the Caribbean is being squeezed between the floor of the Atlantic and an opposing plate in the Pacific. The pressure has piled up the sediment and volcanic activity that created the arcing chain of the Antilles.

The Caribbean islands, excepting Trinidad, have probably never been connected with any continent. The distances between Cuba, the nearest to the mainland, and Florida (90 miles across the Straits of Florida), and between Cuba and Mexico's Yucatán Peninsula (135 miles across the Yucatán Channel), are about the same as those between comparable islands and nearby continents. These straits are both so deep, however, that Cuba probably never had a continental connection even at the height of the glaciation. Most West Indies islands have a sparse fauna, a small selection of the North, Central and South American wildlife. The only vertebrate class that managed to reach the islands in profusion is the reptiles. The islands have land turtles and perhaps a hundred species of lizards, including large iguanas that may reach six feet in length and small anoles that change their color in response to temperature, light and emotional state, and are sold in circuses and pet shops as "chameleons." Cuba, Hispaniola and Jamaica are hosts to the wide-ranging American crocodile, *Crocodylus acutus,* and Cuba also has its own endemic species of croc, *C. rhombifer,* which has been hunted so

Haitian tree snail

much for its hide that there are now only a few thousand individuals left in the swamps of the Zapata Peninsula in southwestern Cuba and on the Isle of Pines. Even snakes have managed to emigrate from the mainlands, although Cuba, the largest of the Indies with more than 20 times the area of Trinidad, has only 16 snake species compared to Trinidad's 38.

One of the most notable differences between Trinidad and the other Caribbean islands is the paucity of native mammals in the rest of the Antilles. While Trinidad has a variety of South American mammals, all of the other islands have little but bats and rodents. Two curious endemic mammals, however, the hutia and the solenodon, have somehow persisted in remote sections of the Greater Antilles, despite the depredations of man and the imported mongoose. The solenodon is a primitive and very rare insectivore, a relative of the tenrec of Madagascar. It looks somewhat like a caricature of a pig, with a long, tapering snout, tiny eyes and nearly naked feet and tail, and it is a native only of Cuba and Hispaniola. Those two islands and Jamaica are the last preserves of the hutia, a rodent that resembles a guinea pig with a small, naked tail. Hutias are highly esteemed for their flesh both by man and introduced animal predators, and they have been hunted to near-extinction. Yet both hutias and solenodons, the only remaining native mammals of the West Indies, survive as rigidly protected relics in the isolation of their islands.

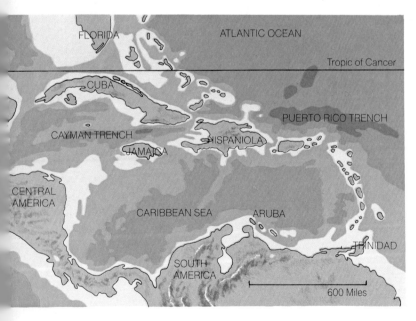

Jungle vegetation crowds the edge of Maracas Bay on Trinidad in the West Indies. Trinidad's plant life, like its animal population, closely resembles that of nearby South America.

50

At Their Own Pace

For all their slow and sluggish ways, land snails are among the most ubiquitous of island colonists. They turn up in great numbers, representing many subspecies on some of the remotest islands in the world—places like Tahiti and Samoa and Hawaii. How did they get to the islands? It is obvious that snails could never have made it on their own, and the answer that most scientists accept is that they arrived as fellow travelers with the birds, in the form of eggs or tiny youngsters the size of wheat grains matted in the plumage or sticking to the muddy feet of avian migrants.

The Caribbean snails have speciated like most of their island brethren to exploit special environments, but retain the basic features of their mainland forebears: two sets of antennae, one with eyes on the tips, spreading mantles that cover their sliding foot, and a strong tendency toward the right. Almost all land snails carry their spirals and most of their vital organs on their right side: The so-called sinistral snails, with whorls on the left, are either rare species or freaks, highly valued by shell collectors.

A small snail hitches a ride on the back of a larger relative (above) in the humid foliage of the National Forest Preserve of Puerto Rico and performs a service in return for the ride, removing algae from the shell of its host with its rasplike tongue, or radula. Many land snails are leaf-eaters and some are destructive of coffee and tobacco plantations.

The shell of a Cuban tree snail (left) is a Mondrian pattern of yellow and white, outlined in thin stripes of mauve. A relative, the Cuban bush snail Polymita picta, has evolved into a number of subspecies with handsome shell markings in a rainbow spectrum of colors.

With its agatelike spirals carried properly to the right, a Jamaican land snail (right) makes its unhurried way across a green stem. Many land snails are edible, highly esteemed by gourmets: During the Napoleonic wars, French soldiers carried cans of escargots with them into battle as emergency rations.

Strophocheilus oblongus, a denizen of the Trinidadian rain forests, lays tiny, half-inch eggs that resemble those of a small bird (below). In its labor, the snail has contorted its shell so that the spirals are on the left side. Some snails are hermaphroditic, simultaneously fertilizing each other's eggs when they breed.

Seemingly in the act of tying itself into a figure eight, the beautifully colored false coral snake at left is a native of Trinidad's rain forest. Except for a yellow collar, it lacks the characteristic yellow bands of its deadly namesake and is a threat only to the small lizards and snakes it feeds on.

The whipsnako, or gray vine snake (below), looks like a Disney caricature of a serpent, with its extremely elongated head, tapered snout and flattened, skinny body. It makes its home in the trees and lianas of the island rain forests, and, while it is mildly venomous, it is not harmful to humans.

The fearsome fer-de-lance (above), named by French settlers for the lancelike shape of its head, is a migrant from Central and South America. It is one of the most widely feared of all venomous snakes.

Serpents of the Isles

In comparison to Trinidad, which abounds in 41 species of snakes, the rest of the Caribbean islands have a relatively small serpentine population that has become even sparser since the arrival of Western colonists and their introduced animals, notably the feral cat and the mongoose. Even so, at least 87 kinds of snakes survive throughout the West Indies, and most are endemic species unique to these islands. Venomous snakes are rare, and only five are dangerous to humans: the bushmaster of Trinidad, which grows to a length of 12 feet and is the world's second largest poisonous snake, after the king cobra; the deadly fer-de-lance (left, below); two coral snakes; and the Aruba rattlesnake, a curiosity that found its sinuous way to that island.

The boa constrictor (right) reaches a length of 18 feet, but is surpassed by a member of the boa family also on Trinidad, the anaconda. A small Cuban relative, *Tropidolphus semicinctus*, has the disconcerting habit of coiling up into a ball and bleeding from the mouth when frightened.

The boa constrictor above, a migrant from the South American mainland, lives in the jungles of Trinidad. Its powerful coils can crush the breath out of small animals but pose little if any threat to humans.

The Cuban parrot (left) is one of the smaller species of parrot found in the West Indies, measuring about 11 to 13 inches. The parrots feed mainly on fruit and annoy the local planters because of the havoc they wreak in the guava and banana plantations.

A Jamaican tody, called Robin Redbreast by local residents, pauses before swallowing a caterpillar (right). Todies are patient hunters of caterpillers and even small lizards. They sit on an exposed branch, waiting, and dart out after their prey. This agile little bird nests in a one-foot-long ground burrow.

These emerald hummingbird nestlings (right) are just beginning to show the vivid green coloring that gives the species its name. The female hummingbird lines her nest with soft plant down and fibers, laying two tiny white eggs inside.

Bird Heaven

The birds of the West Indies are so spectacular both in numbers and in plumage that the area has been called an ornithological paradise. Columbus reported seeing "birds of a thousand kinds" when he arrived on Hispaniola in 1492. Scientists believe that the abundance of bird life is due to the fact that it was relatively easy for birds to cross water gaps between the mainland and the islands—especially in the past when the gaps were smaller.

Some migratory birds, like the osprey, regularly stop over in the islands during their annual winter flight from North America. But many West Indies birds reside there year round. Three of the full-time residents are shown here: the Cuban parrot, the Jamaican tody and the emerald hummingbird. They typify the variety of the avifauna of the West Indies, bearing little resemblance to each other except in their colorful plumage. What they do have in common is that they can be found nowhere else.

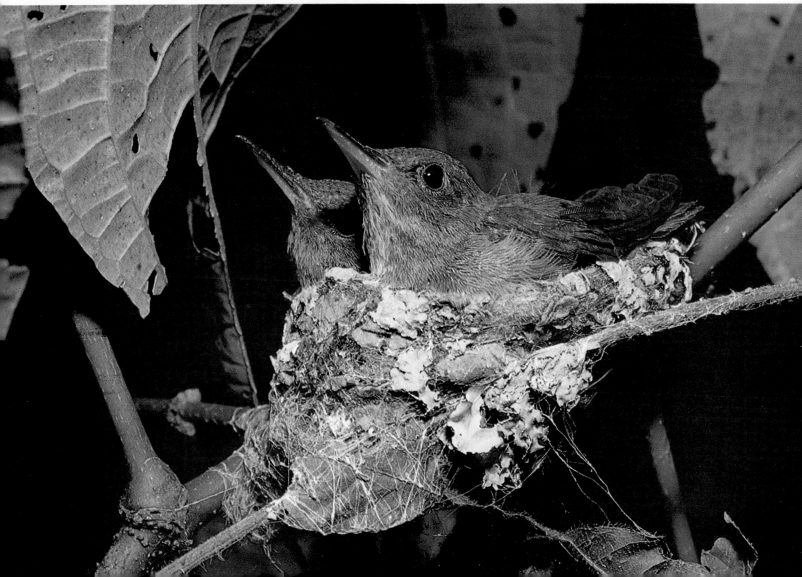

A tiny murine opossum (left) holds on to a flower with its long, hairless, prehensile tail as it peers off the end of a leaf. Often called a mouse opossum because of its appearance and size, a murine opossum is no bigger than a grain of rice when it is born, only 17 days after fertilization. Like all of the marsupials, the young opossum must attach itself to a nipple in its mother's pouch and continue its development outside the womb for about two months.

A collared anteater (right) assumes its upright defense position, balancing on its tail and hind legs so it can slash out with the long, sharp claws on either hand. The anteater uses these same claws to rip open ant or termite nests. It then extends its long, sticky tongue and, when enough insects are trapped on it, sucks the tongue back into its tubular mouth. The anteater has no teeth with which to chew its food. The insects that it eats are ground up in its muscular gizzard for digestion.

Hutias like to huddle not only on rocks (right), but also in the branches of trees. These members of the rodent family vary greatly in color and size from island to island: Some are as large as small dogs, while others are only the size of a guinea pig. Hutias are mainly arboreal and they have a peculiar way of descending from trees: by walking down the trunk headfirst.

Odd West Indians

The collared anteater (above) and the murine opossum (opposite) are native South Americans that have penetrated the West Indies only as far as Trinidad. These and the other Trinidadian mammals may have crossed to the island when it was still connected to the mainland. The presence of the beaverlike hutia, which inhabits the forests of Cuba, the Bahamas, Jamaica and Hispaniola, is more of a mystery, since these islands have probably never been connected to any mainland, and the deep water and strong current that separate them would have prevented any animal from ever crossing over. However the hutia may have arrived, it had no natural predator to contend with until dogs and mongooses were introduced to the islands. These two alien predators have depleted the hutia population to such an extent that the unique mammal is endangered.

Hawaii

Two thousand miles from North America, 3,000 miles from Asia and 4,400 miles from Australia, the Hawaiian Islands —for all their modern importance to man as the crossroads of the Pacific—are among the most isolated places on earth. They are the classic example of islands that are oceanic both geologically and biologically.

Hawaii has never been part of any continent nor connected to any by land bridges. It was born sterile out of the sea, formed entirely of volcanic material spewed forth from underneath the ocean floor in steaming rivers of fire. The principal islands are located over a relatively stationary "hot spot" of molten rock, some 185 miles in diameter, deep beneath the earth's surface. Hawaii also sits on the great Pacific Ocean tectonic plate, which is steadily creeping northwestward toward Asia at a speed of two and a half to three inches a year. As the Pacific plate moves across the hot spot, molten lava periodically breaks through the crust from below and belches forth into the sea.

Over millions of years, such eruptions have—layer upon layer—built up the various Hawaiian Islands. But the steady northwestward drift of the plate eventually carries each of the islands away from the hot spot, and subsequent eruptions break through the plate at a more southeasterly location to form a new island. This motion of the plate has produced a linear chain of 20 islands that today extends some 1,600 miles from Kure and Midway Islands in the northwest along the Leeward Islands to the eight major Hawaiian Islands—Niihau, Kauai, Oahu, Molokai, Lanai, Kahoolawe, Maui and Hawaii—in the southeast.

The native fauna of the Hawaiian Islands consists only of those animals that were able to drift or fly there over the sea. The islands are near enough to one another so that once an animal reached any one, it might easily proceed to the others. In the past there may have been other islands—now sunk beneath the ocean—that might have served animals as stepping-stones. The only land mammal that got to Hawaii without the aid of man is the bat—a single species of *Lasiurus*, which came from America. The islands' 67 endemic species of land birds are believed to be descended from no more than 15 original immigrant species, some from the Americas, others from the remote Melanesian islands or Asia. Of the insular invertebrates, scientists calculate that only 300 original insect species and 24 immigrant land snail species account for all of Hawaii's present populations of native insects and land snails.

Those animals that did make it across 2,000 miles or more of open ocean found themselves on hospitable islands indeed. The Hawaiian Islands generally bask in balmy subtropical weather—the average temperature in Honolulu is in the mid-70s and the northeast trade winds dump a generous rainfall averaging 70 inches a year. But the islands also have extremely rugged topography and high mountains (Hawaii's Mauna Loa and Mauna Kea rise to nearly 14,000 feet and Maui's Haleakala to 10,000 feet). As a result, for islands of relatively modest size, they offer animals a remarkable variety of climates and habitats. Temperatures can go from over 90° F. on the coast to below freezing on snow-clad mountain summits. Mount Waialeale on the island of Kauai, with 451 inches of rain a year, is the wettest spot on earth.

With so many varied and vacant environments, the few animals that did get to the islands evolved almost explosively into new species and fanned out into new habitats, remaining undisturbed by man until the Polynesians colonized the islands over 1,200 years ago. The 24 immigrant land snail species evolved into over 1,000 species; almost every valley, sometimes every tree, on the main islands has its own distinctive form. The original alien insects developed into over 7,000 species, some so highly specialized that they will feed on only a single type of plant. Hawaii has some 100 described species of native spiders, and many still undescribed or unfound. Only recently a strange yellow-green, comb-footed spider was discovered on Oahu. Dozens of variations of these "happy face" spiders (opposite) have turned up since. The survival advantage of its red-and-black Halloween mask is questionable; without it the spider would be almost indiscernible to the human eye, for the creature is almost translucent—and only one eighth of an inch long.

The endemic land birds increased their species into 67 of the most spectacular birds anywhere. The oo, a member of the honey eater family, has bright yellow leg feathers that the Polynesians fashioned into capes, cloaks and head-dresses. One water bird settled down and became a land bird: Geese, apparently, were blown off course and, once established on the islands, evolved into the nene, the Hawaiian state bird, a goose that has adapted to life on the sparsely vegetated lava flows high on the flanks of Mauna Loa and other Hawaiian volcanoes. The colorful honey-creepers, or Drepanididae, are an extraordinary example of

Happy face spider

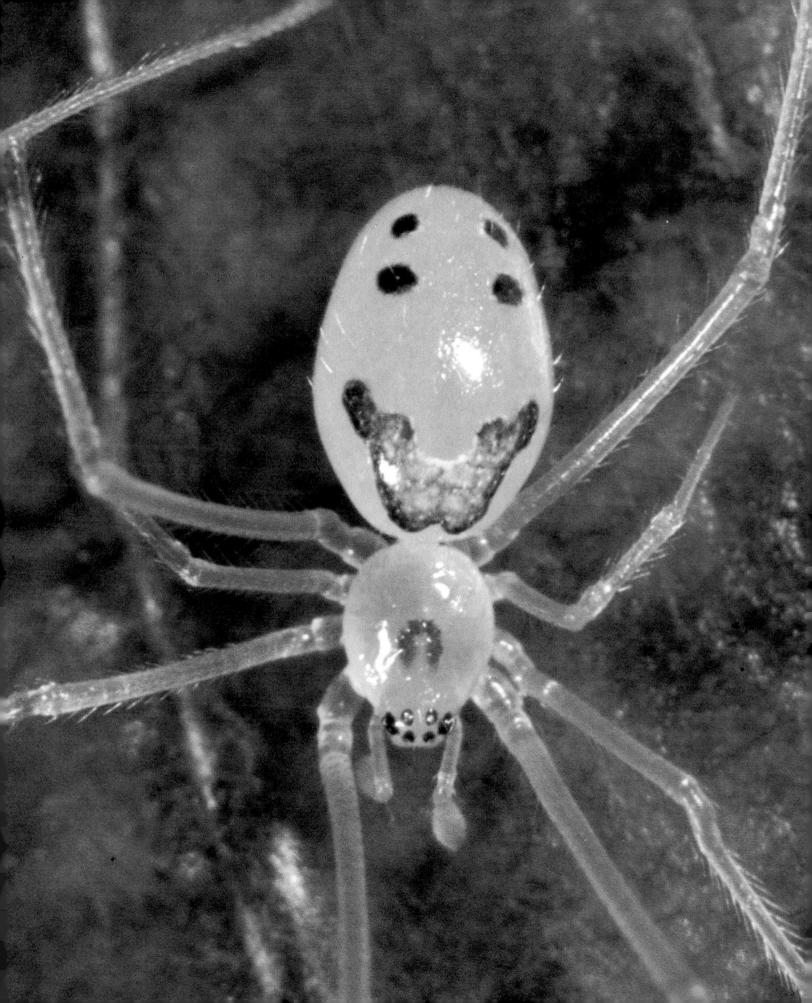

how animals adapt physically to new livelihoods on islands. From a single finch or tanager, 20 or more species
evolved, with different beak shapes specifically suited for
different kinds of diet.

Unfortunately, as is so often the case with island creatures, the Hawaiian birds—which had evolved undisturbed in their protected island haven—proved unable to
compete when Western civilization finally engulfed the
Hawaiian Islands in the wake of Captain James Cook's 1778
visit. Men imported predators—rats, mongooses, cats,
dogs—that devoured birds and their young, and other
animals, such as rabbits, goats, sheep, cattle, pigs, that
trampled nests and ate the plants the birds needed for food.
Another insidious destroyer was the mosquito, which was
inadvertently introduced to Hawaii in 1826. Mosquitoes
transmit avian malaria and bird pox, diseases to which the
Hawaiian birds had had no previous exposure and no im-
munity. Altogether, 23 of the land birds are already extinct,
and another 29 are considered rare or endangered. Many of
the honeycreepers have not been seen in years, and by 1950
the nene population was reduced to 30 birds. The nene's
remarkable comeback has been due in large part to a prodigious gander named Kamehameha, after Hawaii's famous
warrior-king. Exported to an English wildfowl preserve in
1951, he became the progenitor of more than 230 birds,
more than half the world population of nenes at the time
(50 were returned to Hawaii) before his death in 1963. But
Hawaii's other birds have shown no such recuperative
powers, and their extirpation is an unparalleled island
tragedy.

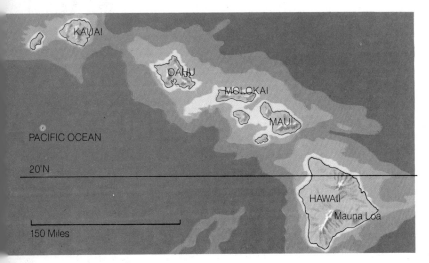

PACIFIC OCEAN

20°N

150 Miles

KAUAI

OAHU

MOLOKAI

MAUI

HAWAII
Mauna Loa

Volcanic scarps swathed in greenery dominate a valley on the
Hawaiian island of Kauai. Deep water surrounding the islands limited
the original populations of endemic species of animals. Those that
have adapted to life on the heights are safest from introduced
predators, pests and man.

Stretched to its full length of one inch, a predaceous caterpillar (right) captures a pomace fly. It will become the adult moth below if it survives its own predators—principally birds. As a protection, the caterpillar has evolved a coloration that camouflages it against the background of the twigs and branches where it waits for its insect prey to come within range of its strike.

A Blackburn's butterfly (left) alights on an aalii plant seed capsule. Females lay their eggs on the plants, and the caterpillars feed on the red seeds. The second species of native Hawaiian butterfly, Kamehameha (below), pauses on a leaf of the mamaki plant.

Beauties and a Beast

Most of the 100,000 species of the world's caterpillars, immature forms of moths and butterflies, are content to be strict vegetarians. But among the caterpillars of Hawaiian moths are such miniature carnivores as the hunter above, right, which shuns all vegetable matter and eats only live prey. It has chewing mouth parts that metamorphose in the adult moth (above, left) into a nectar-siphoning system; the change converts the insect from predator to blossom sipper. The predaceous behavior was first discovered in 1972, when a caterpillar was observed methodically devouring a large, active blowfly.

In contrast to its large endemic moth population of more than 1,000 species, Hawaii has only two species of endemic butterflies. Blackburn's butterfly (opposite) is found throughout the upland regions, and scientists have not yet been definitely able to identify the original species from which it developed. The brilliant Kamehameha at left was first discovered in the early 19th century.

The iiwi (right) with its bright vermilion feathers, salmon-colored bill and vivid orange legs is one of the more flamboyant members of a flamboyant family. The bright red feathers so appealed to the original Polynesian settlers that they once plucked the birds to weave magnificent plumed cloaks and helmets for their kings, a practice long since abandoned.

The apapane (left) braces itself jauntily, extracting every bit of nectar it possibly can from the ohia blossoms it has chosen. The apapane is a very active creature and in flight its wings make a loud, buzzing sound. It usually flies in small flocks.

What the crested honeycreeper (right) lacks in spectacular color, it makes up for with the white, gray or gold fringelike crest above its beak. It is larger than most of the other honeycreepers, with charcoal gray and orange plumage. Perching high above the forest floor, it appears a lord of all it surveys.

True to the meaning of the Polynesian word kihi ("curved"), the amakihi (right), strikingly plumed in lime-green and yellow, uses its bending bill as a tiny probe to dig in the crevices of bark and in folded leaves for insect provender.

Honeycreepers

The brightly colored little creatures on these pages are not to be satisfied with a diet of nectar only, despite their name and the profusion of Hawaiian blossoms. The honeycreepers are endemic to Hawaii, having evolved from a single species, and have adapted beautifully to a varied diet—some have delicate curved bills to probe for nectar and some have stouter bills to probe for insects. Over thousands of centuries, the island's lush vegetation, fruit and insects reinforced the comfort of a safe, unchallenging world for the little birds, but this has changed: Since the arrival of man, 15 varieties have become extinct.

To dip into bell-shaped, nectar-producing flowers, the iiwi has a long, downcurved bill, perfectly adapted to the flower's form. However, the iiwi also feeds on caterpillars

and fruit flies, keeping an alert eye out for them in the lobeloid—an indigenous plant. The apapane (opposite, center) is the most conspicuous species of honeycreeper, nesting in the top of the ohia trees, in tree-fern fronds or in the hollows of the porous lava rock. The apapane varies its diet of nectar with insects and caterpillars. The bill of the amakihi (opposite, bottom) is shorter and noticeably less curved than those of some of the other honeycreepers, and the birds's staple diet is insects. One of the rarest of these exquisite creatures is the crested honeycreeper (above). Living in forest areas 6,000 feet above sea level, it is found only on the island of Maui. As if to resist impending extinction, it is an aggressive bird, often dominating other species in the neighborhood.

A Trio of Rarities

Among the rarest Hawaiian birds are a raptor, a dry-land goose and an elegant wader. Fewer than 500 of the imposing native hawks (opposite) remain in the lofty, mountainous forests. Soaring gracefully in frequent free-spirited airborne displays, they remain alert to home in on the vulnerable birds, insects and small rodents they feed on, a valuable service in keeping such pests under control.

Captive breeding has saved the Hawaiian goose, or nene (above), and new breeding stock has assured them of a future in the Hawaiian ecology. Though they once raised their young in the moist, grassy lowlands, the few nenes remaining in the wild now live in dry, mountainous regions, feeding on berries and succulent plants. The stilt (right) was a game bird but is now protected by law, and 1,500 or so of the long-legged waders still breed and nest in the island mudflats, marshes and ponds.

Two banded nenes (left) roam freely through a government-financed Hawaiian sanctuary. The feet of these geese are no longer completely webbed, as the big birds have forsaken the water's edge to settle inland on mountainous regions far from the dangers of civilization.

A Hawaiian stilt (left) stands daintily on one leg, alert for the sight of the small fish and crustaceans it feeds on. In flight the stilt is ponderous, flapping its wings slowly with its long legs outstretched behind.

A Hawaiian hawk; or io (its native name approximates its piercing cry), scans the forest (right), on guard for any movement signaling the presence of prey. When it sights a possible target, the hawk descends like a lightning bolt, its hooked bill and sharp-edged claws poised for the kill.

The Galápagos

After the Spanish first came upon the fog-shrouded islands in the early 16th century, they gave them two names: Las Islas Galápagos (the tortoise islands), after their giant land tortoises, and Las Islas Encantadas (the bewitched or enchanted islands) because they had so much trouble locating them again that they thought the islands must have moved about in the sea. Three hundred years later when Charles Darwin visited the Galápagos, he was enchanted by "the amount of creative force . . . displayed on these small, barren and rocky islands." And today modern naturalists are still enchanted. Says zoologist Ian Thornton: "The Galápagos Islands can . . . lay claim to being the birthplace of modern biology."

Like the Hawaiian Islands, the Galápagos are clearly oceanic in every sense of the word. Also like Hawaii, the Galápagos are entirely volcanic but even younger, perhaps no more than two million years old. And, although their wildlife was more recently acquired, it found its way to the Galápagos more easily since the South American continent is just 600 miles away. Animals have one direct means of transportation available for covering those 600 miles. The islands are in the path of the Humboldt Current, which curves westward from the coast of Ecuador.

Scientists have calculated that a natural raft of tangled vegetation might make the journey in about two weeks. Any animal that made it alive, however, would find an environment much less hospitable than that of Hawaii. The Galápagos archipelago is an irregular cluster of 16 islands and assorted islets and rocks, straddling the equator and scattered over 36,000 square miles of the Pacific Ocean. The climate of the islands, moreover, is far from typically equatorial. Average monthly air temperatures range from 70° to 83° F., and the coastal areas of the islands get only three or four inches of rain a year. The lower elevations of the islands are covered with cacti and thorny shrubs, and the higher elevations, which tend to be better watered, are densely wooded.

The Galápagos have nevertheless accumulated a significantly larger collection of land animals than Hawaii, all of them from South or Central America—with the sole exception of a land mollusk that is of Polynesian origin, 3,000 miles away. The Galápagos have few mammals. There is one genus of bat (the same intrepid species that made it to Hawaii) and five species of rice rat. The Galápagos rats, Ian Thornton points out, hold the terrestrial world record for crossing seawater. Of the 89 species and subspecies of birds that nest in the islands, 77 are endemic.

It is the reptiles, as Charles Darwin reported, that give "the most striking character to the zoology of these islands. The species are not numerous, but the numbers of individuals of each species are extraordinarily great."

In addition to the famous giant land tortoises, there are geckos, small and brightly colored lava lizards and even a harmless brown snake, plus two large iguanas, each three to four feet long and each endemic to the islands. One of them lives and feeds on land. "I cannot give a more forcible proof of their numbers," Darwin wrote in *The Voyage of the Beagle*, "than by stating that when we were left at James Island, we could not for some time find a spot free from their burrows on which to pitch our single tent." (Today, there are no land iguanas at all on James Island; all have been destroyed by imported domestic pigs.)

The other large iguana is a seagoing version, the only marine lizard in the world. Biologists believe that it has almost certainly evolved from the land iguana. Although the marine iguana sleeps on land, it feeds in the sea, swimming out hundreds of yards from shore, diving to depths of 35 feet to graze on seaweed.

Darwin was fascinated to learn that the different islands of the archipelago "to a considerable extent are inhabited by a different set of beings." The inhabitants told him that they could distinguish the giant tortoises from the various islands. Those from Charles and Hood islands in the southern part of the archipelago have "their shells in front thick and turned up like a Spanish saddle, whilst the tortoises from James Island are rounder, blacker and have a better taste when cooked." The tortoises are now extinct on at least three of the islands and are endangered on many others. In recent years, scientists have been making efforts to restore the populations. The Bronx Zoo has returned an adult female, young tortoises have been bred at the San Diego Zoo, and an extensive breeding program is underway at the Charles Darwin Research Station in the Galápagos themselves.

Darwin was also intrigued by a group of a dozen or so species of finches that are now known as Darwin's finches. The dark, sparrow-sized birds are obviously related, and today they are recognized as all descended from a single common ancestor and as a classic example of how animals radiate in their physical form as they adapt to new ways of

Marine iguanas

making their living on islands. The finches developed new beak shapes as they found new diets. One feeds on cactus flowers and seeds and has developed a long, somewhat curved bill. Another feeds on leaves and moderately hard seeds and has evolved a thick, sturdy bill. And one finch has moved into the empty woodpecker niche and probes for insects in the cracks and crevices of trees. It did not develop a woodpeckerlike bill and tongue, however, but became one of the few birds in the world to employ a tool. It selects a small stick or cactus thorn and manipulates it with its beak to extract its dinner from the bark. The finches helped to undermine Darwin's faith in the theory of independent creation: "Seeing this gradation and diversity of structure in one small, intimately related group of birds, one might really fancy that from an original paucity of birds in this archipelago, one species had been taken and modified for different ends."

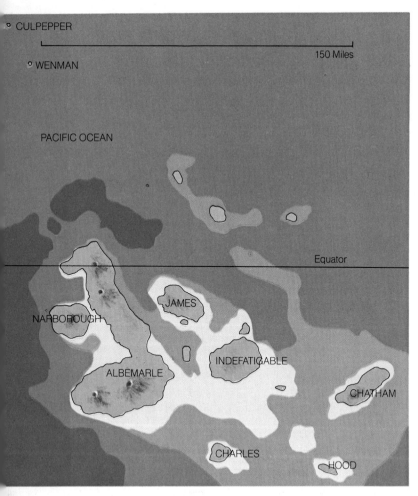

Pyramidal mounds of lava rise from the islet of Bartholomew (foreground) and James Island in the Galápagos. Proximity of South America accounts for both the origin of the islands' wildlife and their volcanism—a byproduct of spreading tectonic plates in the Pacific.

Spines of the prickly pear cactus are no problem for the sharp-toothed land iguanas above, which nonchalantly consume the entire plant, thorns and all, with no ill effects.

Marine iguanas (left) share close quarters on a rocky promontory. Long, sharp claws help them get a solid grip on underwater rocks where the kelp and algae are rich.

The land iguana at right confidently surveys its territory. Burrows are often dug on the lava rim of an extinct volcano.

Docile Dragons

The soft, craggy lava rocks of the Galápagos shore support a large population of marine iguanas that are found nowhere else on earth, as well as less unusual land iguanas that never go near the water. The isolated archipelago is free from predators except for gulls, Galápagos hawks and dogs, which are a serious threat to the lizards. The adult iguanas, three or four feet long, with crested heads and long serpentine tails, roam freely around their islands without fear, congregating in large groups on the rocks during the day in the hot equatorial sun and often accompanied by red crabs (overleaf). After sundown, the dragon-like creatures retreat to shallow burrows.

Marine iguanas (below, opposite) are the only lizards in the world that venture into the sea. With their short, blunt snouts and sharp teeth they graze the surface of underwater rocks. They have been observed submerging for as long as 50 minutes to feed on the kelp on the sea floor. Excess salt accumulated in their underwater forays is collected in a special pair of glands and spewed from the creature's nostrils in the best dragon fashion when it is out of the water. When contesting territory, an iguana adopts a stiff-legged stance, its crest of dorsal scales erect, throat bloated and body size appreciably increased. Bobbing its head up and down, it uses the cone-shaped scales atop its head to butt its rival. But for all their menacing appearance, iguanas rarely harm each other: Their battles are mock combats designed to intimidate rather than kill or maim.

Two combative red crabs (left) square off for a sparring match. The brightly patterned red-and-blue crabs, with their unmistakable stalk eyes, wander about foraging in tidal pools along the Galápagos shoreline.

As a helpful hitchhiker, a Galápagos crab rides on the back of a marine iguana (opposite, above). The crabs clamber onto the iguanas' backs as they emerge from the sea and remove ticks and other harmful parasites from their scaly skins.

Scuttling over the hard, black lava
rock the red crabs (left) seem unaware
of the dragonlike creatures towering
over them. Infrequently an iguana
swims too far out to sea and drowns,
and the crabs then feast on the
beached carcass. Consuming a more
usual meal, the scavenger above
grasps a dead squid with its pincers.

Galápagos tortoises gather to drink and wallow in a pool fed by a freshwater upland spring (left). A tortoise drinks with its head submerged up to the eyes, swallowing about ten mouthfuls per minute. Pools are also used by tortoises to protect their soft parts from mosquitoes. If no pool exists, the tortoise creates one by churning up grass and mud around a spring with its powerful forelegs.

The head of a Galápagos tortoise (below) contains no teeth. The creature must rely upon its sharp-edged jaws—which clamp together like scissors to nip the grass, berries and even prickly pear cactus that are the mainstays of its diet. It is not unwilling to scavenge bits of a dead animal or even prey on a small live one. But the most remarkable thing about the tortoise's diet is that it can stay alive for months without eating anything at all.

Ancient Voyagers

The presence of the giant tortoise on the Galápagos Islands is no great mystery. The first of these hardy reptiles probably swam or drifted over from the mainland. Tortoises can go without food or drinking water for lengthy periods and can float in salt water without ill effect. Harmless to man, the armored behemoth—weighing up to 600 pounds—will tuck its head inside its shell with a hiss when approached. But during mating season male tortoises often attack each other, smashing their heads together or charging each other and retracting their heads at the last minute.

The female tortoise lays up to nine eggs in a deep mudhole, where they take about 13 months to hatch. Even after hatching, though, survival is a chancy matter, since many babies are trapped inside the nest hole by hardened mud, and most of those that do dig their way out are likely to be devoured by waiting gulls and herons.

The Encantadas
by Herman Melville

In 1841 Herman Melville joined a whaling expedition to the South Pacific, a voyage that was the prelude to his enduring masterwork, Moby Dick. *His trip took him around Cape Horn and up the South American coast to the Galápagos Islands, where he encountered the fabled giant tortoises. In 1853 Melville was commissioned to write a novel about the great land turtles. Instead, he wrote a series of sketches, which includes the following.*

Most ugly shapes and horrible aspects,
Such as Dame Nature selfe mote feare to see,
Or shame, that ever should so fowle defects
From her most cunning hand escaped bee;
All dreadfull pourtraicts of deformitee:
Ne wonder, if these do a man appall;
For all that here at home we dreadfull hold,
Be but as bugs to fearen babes withall,
Compared to the creatures in these isles' entrall.

"Feare nought," then saide the Palmer well aviz'd,
"For these same monsters are not these in deed,
But are into these fearfull shapes diguiz'd."
And lifting up his vertuous staffe on hye,
Then all that dreadful armie fast can flye
Into great Tethys bosome, where they hidden lye.

In view of the description given, may one be gay upon the Encantadas? Yes: that is, find one the gaiety, and he will be gay. And, indeed, sackcloth and ashes as they are, the isles are not perhaps unmitigated gloom. For while no spectator can deny their claims to a most solemn and superstitious consideration, no more than my firmest resolutions can decline to behold the spectre-tortoise when emerging from its shadowy recess; yet even the tortoise, dark and melancholy as it is upon the back, still possesses a bright side; its calipee or breast-plate being sometimes a faint yellowish or golden tinge. Moreover, every one knows that tortoises as well as turtles are such a make, that if you but put them on their backs you thereby expose their bright sides without the possibility of their recovering themselves, and turning into view the other. But after you have done this, and because you have done this, you should not swear that the tortoise has no dark side. Enjoy the bright, keep it turned up perpetually if you can, but be honest, and don't deny the black. Neither should he, who cannot turn the tortoise from its natural position so as to hide the darker and expose his livelier aspect, like a great October pumpkin in the sun, for that cause declare the creature to be one total inky blot. The tortoise is both black and bright. But let us to particulars.

Some months before my first stepping ashore upon the group, my ship was cruising in its close vicinity. One noon we found ourselves off the South Head of Albermarle, and not very far from the land. Partly by way of freak, and partly by way of spying out so strange a country, a boat's crew was sent ashore, with orders to see all they could, and besides, bring back whatever tortoises they could conveniently transport.

It was after sunset, when the adventurers returned. I looked down over the ship's high side as if looking down over the curb of a well, and dimly saw the damp boat deep in the sea with some unwonted weight. Ropes were dropt over, and presently three huge antediluvian-looking tortoises, after much straining, were landed on deck. They seemed hardly of the seed of earth. We had been abroad upon the waters for five long months, a period amply sufficient to make all things of the land wear a fabulous hue to the dreamy mind. Had three Spanish custom-house officers boarded us then, it is not unlikely that I should have curiously stared at them, felt of them, and stroked them much as savages serve civilized guests. But instead of three custom-house officers, behold these really wondrous tortoises—none of your schoolboy mud-turtles—but black as widower's weeds, heavy as chests of plate, with vast shells medallioned and orbed like shields, and dented and blistered like shields that have breasted a battle, shaggy, too, here and there, with dark green moss, and slimy with the spray of the sea. These mystic creatures, suddenly translated by night from unutterable solitudes to our peopled deck, affected me in a manner not easy to unfold. They seemed newly crawled forth from beneath the foundations of the world. Yea, they seemed the identical tortoises whereon the Hindoo plants this total sphere. With a lantern I inspected them more closely. Such worshipful venerableness of aspect! Such furry greenness mantling the rude peelings and healing the fissures of their shattered shells. I no more saw three tortoises. They expanded—became transfigured. I seemed to see three Roman Coliseums in magnificent decay.

Ye oldest inhabitants of this, or any other isle, said I, pray, give me the freedom of your three walled towns.

The great feeling inspired by these creatures was that of age:—dateless, indefinite endurance. And, in fact, that any other creature can live and breathe as long as the tortoise of the Encantadas, I will not readily believe. Not to hint of their known capacity of sustaining life, while going without food for an entire year, consider that impregnable armor of their living mail. What other bodily being possesses such a citadel wherein to resist the assaults of Time?

As lantern in hand, I scraped among the moss and beheld the ancient scars of bruises received in many a sullen fall among the marly mountains of the isle—scars strangely widened, swollen, half obliterate, and yet distorted like those sometimes found in the bark of very hoary trees, I seemed an antiquary of a geologist, studying the birdtracks and ciphers upon the exhumed slates trod by incredible creatures whose very ghosts are now defunct.

As I lay in my hammock that night, overhead I heard the slow weary draggings of the three ponderous strangers along the encumbered deck. Their stupidity or their resolution was so great, that they never went aside for any impediment. One ceased his movements altogether just before the mid-watch. At sunrise I found him butted like a battering-ram against the immovable foot of the foremast, and still striving, tooth and nail, to force the impossible passage. That these tortoises are the victims of a penal, or malignant, or perhaps a downright diabolical enchanter, seems in nothing more likely than in that strange infatuation of hopeless toil which so often possesses them. I have

known them in their journeyings ram themselves heroically against rocks, and long abide there, nudging, wriggling, wedging, in order to displace them, and so hold on their inflexible path. Their crowning curse is their drudging impulse to straightforwardness in a belittered world.

Meeting with no such hinderance as their companion did, the other tortoises merely fell foul of small stumbling-blocks—buckets, blocks, and coils of rigging—and at times in the act of crawling over them would slip with an astounding rattle to the deck. Listening to these draggings and concussions, I thought me of the haunt from which they came; an isle full of metallic ravines and gulches, sunk bottomlessly into the hearts of splintered mountains, and covered for many miles with inextricable thickets. I then pictured these three straightforward monsters, century after century, writhing through the shades, grim as blacksmiths; crawling so slowly and ponderously, that not only did toad-stools and all fungous things grow beneath their feet, but a sooty moss sprouted upon their backs. With them I lost myself in volcanic mazes; brushed away endless boughs of rotting thickets; till finally in a dream I found myself sitting cross-legged upon the foremost, a Brahmin similarly mounted upon either side, forming a tripod of foreheads which upheld the universal cope.

Such was the wild nightmare begot by my first impression of the Encantadas tortoise. But next evening, strange to say, I sat down with my shipmates, and made a merry repast from tortoise steaks and tortoise stews; and supper over, out knife, and helped convert the three mighty concave shells into three fanciful soup-tureens, and polished the three flat yellowish calipees into three gorgeous salvers.

81

Known by Their Bills

Thirteen species of finch are endemic to the Galápagos Islands, but all are descended from a common ancestor and share a common name: Darwin's finch. Each species has evolved a slightly different beak, and it was by beak shape and size that Charles Darwin distinguished one from another when he visited the islands in 1835.

The birds themselves sometimes have difficulty telling one another apart, since all have similar dark coloration that merges with the island's lava crags (below). They solve the dilemma by close-up inspection of one another's beaks, a foolproof identification test. A pair of finches will often feed each other, a form of finch affection.

One species of Darwin's finch, aptly named the cactus ground finch, builds its nest in the prickly pear cactus. The cactus also provides the finch with a food source. The cactus ground finch's beak is longer and slenderer than those of most finches, enabling the bird to probe inside a cactus blossom for the sticky material within. And because its beak is stronger than those of most flower feeders, the bird can break thick fruit skin to extract the seeds.

A flower-feeding finch (left) prepares to probe deep into the yellow flowers of the prickly pear cactus with its specially adapted slender beak.

The cactus ground finch below has submerged its entire head in a cactus blossom and emerged with head feathers and beak flecked with yellow pollen. When a bird sips the viscous green fluid of the cactus fruit its feathers often become matted with a sticky film. In order to clean them the finch simply rubs its head against a bit of lava.

83

Sea Lions in the Sun

A sea lion on a tropical island would appear to be a contradiction in terms. Nevertheless, the cow and her pup at right are perfectly at home lounging beneath a Galápagos cactus. Warm-blooded mammals, the sea lions actually enjoy the balmy airs of the tropics, although they probably first arrived on the islands when the surrounding Pacific waters were much colder than they are today. And they still depend on the relatively cool Humboldt Current, which flows north from Antarctica, to provide them with the fish that are the staple of their diet.

The mother and pup here are secluded in the shade to escape the Galápagos sun. However, sea lions are herd animals, and often one bull presides over as many as 30 females and their young. Yet many males must live alone most of their lives, since the only way for a bull to get a harem of cows is to steal or win them in battle from another bull. A bull will bellow ferociously and charge if he mistakes a human intruder for a challenger who is after his cows. But such bellicosity is often only a show. Most of the time sea lions are extremely friendly, and man is usually regarded as just another strange playmate. In fact, the bull sea lion is quite domestic. He spends most of his day breaking up squabbles between his various mates and taking a share in the raising and protection of the pups.

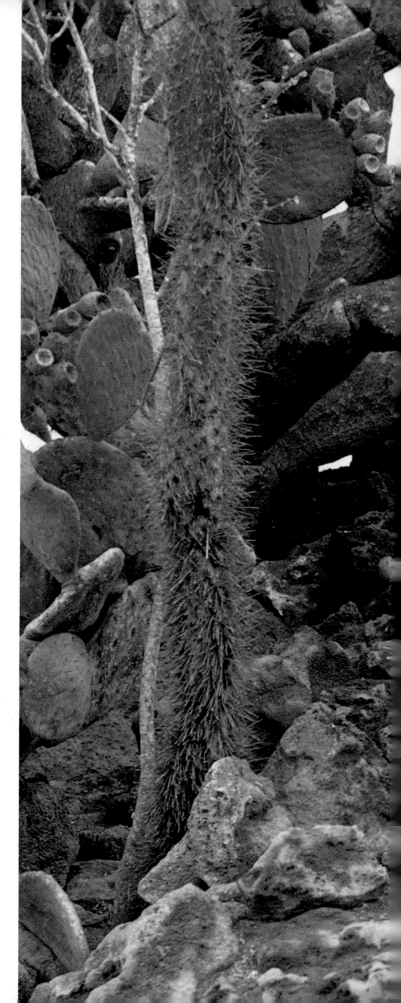

The Indonesian Archipelago

The elongated cluster of islands that stretches eastward from Sumatra to New Guinea and north to the Philippines, separating the Indian Ocean from the Pacific and nearly connecting southeast Asia with Australia, is the largest archipelago on earth. Some 3,800 miles in length and 2,200 from north to south, the Indonesian, or Malay, archipelago reaches nearly one sixth of the way around the globe and is made up of thousands upon thousands of islands, including the world's second and third largest (New Guinea, 304,200 square miles, and Borneo, 286,969 square miles). Sprawled almost entirely within the tropics (the equator bisects Borneo), these islands have a steady, humid climate, with annual temperatures that average 80° F. and abundant rainfall that mists most of the islands and creates lush rain forests. In their animal life, the storied East Indies are the richest, most complex of all island groups.

The islands are perched on the trembling edge of a vast crater, the Pacific Ocean, which, at 70 million square miles, is the largest body of water on earth. Most of the Pacific Ocean floor is a mighty tectonic plate, moving inexorably westward and casting off a loop of earthquakes and volcanic eruptions around its perimeter—a so-called "ring of fire"—as its edges crunch against other plates. Indonesia, which forms a bend of the loop, is the most volcanic region on earth—a dubious claim to fame that was confirmed in modern times by the violent upheaval of Krakatoa (page 15).

The enormous archipelago divides into two distinct continental shelf regions separated by deep seas. New Guinea and its satellite islands sit on the Australian shelf and were once connected to Australia by land. As a consequence, their animal populations, including the distinctive marsupials, are much like those of Australia. In the central region of the archipelago, Celebes and the Moluccas are surrounded by deep sea channels and have probably never been connected to the other islands. Celebes (69,277 square miles) is unique among all insular habitats, according to zoologist Philip Darlington, "in completely lacking fishes of strictly fresh water families while having several large mammals." Two of Celebes' mammal species are marsupials from Australia; some are southeast Asian immigrants, while a large number of them are endemic species found nowhere else.

An endemic buffalo occurs on Mindoro, one of the 7,000 islands of the Philippines, a triangular group on the north-ern edge of the archipelago. The Philippines sit uneasily on the rim of the Mindoro Trench, a deep abyss formed by the forward edge of the Pacific plate. The Philippines' mammals migrated from southeast Asia by way of Indonesia along land bridges during the Ice Ages. Thus, the southern Philippines are the homes of civets, monkeys and the spotted deer, and Palawan has a badger, an otter and the freakish, hairy binturong.

In Indonesia proper, the large islands of Sumatra, Borneo and Java rise from the shallow (150 feet deep) Sunda shelf and were part of the mainland until very recent times, which accounts for their abundant and varied fauna, and its general similarity to that of southeast Asia. Farther east in Indonesia, there occurs one of the world's sharpest breaks between two major zoological regions. This schism appears between the western and central zones of the archipelago, and is demarcated by the narrow, 20-mile strait that separates the islands of Bali and Lombok. It is a zoological barrier known as Wallace's Line, after the 19th century naturalist Alfred Russel Wallace, who was the first to discern it. "We may pass in two hours from one great division of the earth to another, differing as essentially in their animal life as Europe does from America," Wallace wrote in his classic volume, *The Malay Archipelago*. "If we travel from Java or Borneo to Celebes or the Moluccas, the difference is still more striking. In the first, the forests abound in monkeys of many kinds, wild cats, deer, civets, and otters, and numerous varieties of squirrels are constantly met with. In the latter, none of these occur."

That mysterious, invisible barrier separating the island fauna so emphatically is nothing less than the dividing line between two continental shelves. Wallace knew nothing of the theory of drifting continents, which was not advanced until more than a half a century after his 1854–1862 explorations. Yet he could observe that all of those islands which lay in the relatively shallow waters within a 100-fathom line around Australia were populated with animals like Australia's own, and he reasoned that they had originated in that unique continent. He also noted that the fauna of the Indonesian islands closest to Australia most nearly resembled the Down Under birds and beasts—mound builders, cockatoos and marsupials—even though the physical appearance of all the islands from east to west was remarkably similar. The farther away from Australia he was, the fainter were the likenesses of life forms to those of that continent.

Then, to the west of Wallace's Line, all reference to Australia abruptly vanished: The wildlife was unmistakably Asian.

That is the reason why the big islands west of the Line are the homes of the most spectacular menagerie of large animals of any island group in the world. The Asian elephant, smaller and more docile than his African counterpart, lumbers through the rain forests of Sumatra and Borneo. Relations of the Bengal tiger were able to island-hop along the archipelago as far east as Bali. The insular counterpart of the Asian leopard lives only on the island of Java, and the rare clouded leopard on Sumatra and Borneo. Two rhinoceroses are native to the larger East Indies, the one-horned rhino of Java, a smaller version of the great Indian rhino, and the even smaller two-horned species of Sumatra and Borneo, weighing just one ton. Sumatra is also the habitat of the tapir, whose closest relatives live on the mainland and half a world away in South America. There are also many monkeys and apes in these westerly islands, including two large primates that exist nowhere else: the comical proboscis monkey, a long-nosed native of Borneo, and the red-haired orangutan (meaning "man of the forest" in Malay) of Borneo and Sumatra.

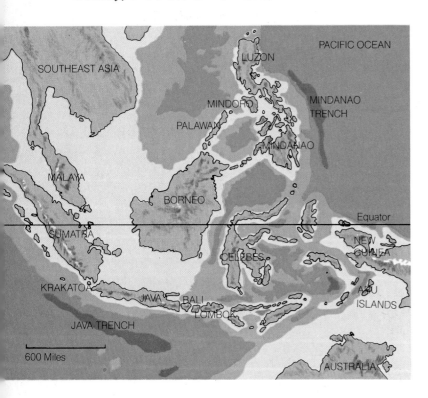

Fruiting spikes of a native grass mask the view of Indian Ocean waters off Sumatra in the Indonesian archipelago. Closest of all of the Indonesian islands to the Asian mainland, Sumatra was probably among the first to attract Asian animals emigrating from Malaya.

Models for Primates

Fossil remains from the Paleocene epoch (about 60 million years ago) suggest that the primate order probably originated in the European-North American area. In succeeding ages, early primates extended their range around the globe. The lemuroids flourished in Madagascar (pages 20–31), while other prosimians took up residence in the forests of southern Asia, Africa and Indonesia.

Among these are the tree shrews (below), so-called "model forms" of the ancestral animal from which the primates originated. Although its classification as a primate still stirs debate because its claw-tipped digits and dependence on its sense of smell are more typical of insectivores than primates, the tree shrew does have many simian attributes, including a relatively large brain case, eye sockets completely encircled by bone and a primarily arboreal life-style.

Higher up the evolutionary ladder are the slothlike lorises (opposite). Unlike tree shrews, these slow-moving arboreal creatures have opposable thumbs and first toes that are virtually at right angles to the rest of their digits, ensuring them of a good grasp in the trees. The tarsier (right) is closer still to the monkeys. Almost all its digits have nails instead of claws, and all are tipped with soft, disklike pads, which provide an excellent nonslip grip.

The startled eyes of the tarsier (above) seem to take up its entire face as it chews on a gecko, and indeed it has the largest orbs in the entire primate order. Keen eyesight and an acute sense of hearing are indispensable equipment for the tarsier's nocturnal way of life.

The tree shrew's pointed snout (left) suggests its dependence on its sense of smell. These diurnal animals are swift runners and able climbers that feed primarily on fruits and insects.

Two hungry slow lorises (opposite) focus their wide-eyed attention on a ripe banana. Nocturnal animals, lorises often hang upside down from branches, freeing their grasping hands for feeding.

A gibbon (right) relaxes between bursts of acrobatics. The smallest of the great apes, standing only three feet tall and weighing only 25 pounds, the gibbon is the only ape that does not build a nest, preferring to huddle in a group when it sleeps.

A proboscis monkey (below) clings to a tree in its Bornean jungle home. The proboscis monkey is primarily a leaf eater, although fruit and flowers are also acceptable food. Most active during the early morning, a proboscis monkey takes readily to the water and often swims and cavorts in rivers and swamps.

Lords of the Trees

Indonesia's lush forests provide the perfect backdrops for the arboreal primates seen on these pages. The gibbon (opposite, top) is a sociable animal that lives in family groups. Each group defines its territorial boundaries with loud hoots that echo through the jungle. The gibbon is the most accomplished aerialist of the great apes, which include the gorilla, the chimpanzee and the orangutan. With arms proportionately longer than those of any other apes, the gibbon uses a deft, hand-over-hand motion called brachiation to swing through the forest canopy, and it can effortlessly span distances of over 30 feet in a single leap.

The fleshy nose of the male proboscis monkey (opposite, bottom), develops only when it is an adult. Males produce a distinctive honking sound that warns other members of the tribe of impending danger. The turned-up nose of the female proboscis is much smaller, and she emits a softer noise. The orangutan (right) also proclaims its whereabouts with a loud call that can be heard for a mile. To preserve their solitary dominion over their territories, males use their voices to warn away rivals.

An orangutan stares placidly from its treetop home (above). Unlike the high-swinging gibbon, the orangutan is an ape that travels through the jungle in a slow, deliberate manner, moving cautiously along a branch as it forages for fruit, leaves, seeds, bark and small birds and eggs.

In Search of the Red Ape

by John MacKinnon

An apprenticeship with zoologist Jane Goodall when she was studying chimpanzees in Tanzania whetted the interest of John MacKinnon in the primates. In the late 1960s, MacKinnon, a young English naturalist, traveled to Sumatra and Borneo to observe the rarest of the great apes, the orangutan. In the following excerpt from his book, In Search of the Red Ape, *he describes the contest between a tribe of orangs and a group of smaller siamangs for possession of a fig tree.*

For the first day things warmed up gradually. One by one other orangs found the juicy harvest and a succession of black faces appeared, ate their fill and moved on again. Towards evening a bunch of hornbills and a troop of long-tailed macaques joined in the celebration and the great tree swayed with their movement.

Next morning the orangs, two young males, two females and a juvenile, were breakfasting early. More hornbills and two giant squirrels kept them company. The orang-utans fed slowly and peacefully until the arrival of a small, dusky male. He mounted a long, sloping branch but somehow incurred the wrath of one of the larger males already in residence. The great bully turned on the newcomer and chased him, squealing, from the tree and across the hillside. The pursuit continued for some considerable distance with the two males careering round in a wide

circle only yards apart. It seemed as though the pursuer would catch his quarry but suddenly he lost interest, their paths separated and the victorious male returned to the repast.

All was peaceful again but not for long. With wild leaping and much shaking of branches a family of five siamangs came hurtling through the canopy and halted opposite the fruit tree. Now, at last, I might see how siamangs and orangs got along together. The siamangs had obviously been attracted by the rich crop but would they dare to sample it when several large orang-utans were in splendid residence?

I did not have to wait long. With a mighty bound the male siamang leapt across into the lowest branch of the fig and was immediately followed by his family. Harrying the other diners they wove to and fro, skipping nimbly from one branch to the next and plucking the yellow fruit as they went. The elderly female was hampered by the tiny coal-black infant clinging to her lap but she easily outpaced the swiftest orang. Suddenly, without any warning, the four adult siamangs swooped in unison on a baby orang-utan who was playing happily by himself. His screams of fear brought his mother rushing to his defence and the evil black apes scattered. Furious, the red female gathered up her frightened baby and, hugging him fiercely to her, carried him out of the danger zone. As though upset by this incident, the orangs began to drift away until soon only one young male was left munching on the lowest bough. The siamangs were determined not to miss this chance and attacked again, four dark furies rushing down on the surprised orang. Clumsily he dashed to the end of the branch and with a hasty backward glance over his

shoulder leaped into mid-air to avoid the vengeful terrors. He crashed into a tree below, landing badly, and hurried for a secure crotch to lick his wounds and wait for the hateful siamangs to leave.

The siamangs, however, took their time. When they had gorged themselves on the sweet figs they settled down to rest. The baby played alongside his mother but his movements were very unsteady and suggested he was only a few months old. I was amazed by what I had seen. I would never have suspected that a band of siamangs could put the much larger orangs to flight but by constant harassment and unexpectedly picking on young or solitary animals they had clearly won the day. This was one rival with which the Bornean red apes did not have to contend.

More amazing sights were in store. When a nearby fig ripened a few days later I was able to break all records for orang watching. My red friends had found the rich crop before me and there were already four large, leafy nests high among the branches. The tree was still thickly covered in figs, however, and there were no orang-utans in sight. It was midday and stiflingly hot. Then I spotted a tuft of bright red hair poking out above the brim of the lowest nest. For an hour nothing happened and then a chin appeared, a chin so broad and distinctive that there was no doubting its owner. Faithful old Redbeard was right at the centre of things again. He took his time to emerge but gradually his magnificent form hove into view. Hanging by one arm he swung leisurely out on to a peripheral bough as though his two hundred pounds' weight was of no consequence. Sampling only the ripest fruit he worked his way steadily along the branch. Contentedly full, he retired to his couch for a well-earned rest. So the day passed in an interminable series of tasty snacks and short naps. In the cool evening a flock of pigeons joined him, fluttering and cooing as they tucked into the ample feast. As the sky darkened the birds departed and I expected Redbeard to wander off and build a night nest in a smaller tree. But instead of descending he inspected his old sleeping quarters and finally settled for the accommodation he had used throughout the day.

By first light the huge tree was alive with feeding animals. Redbeard sat enthroned among the branches and eyed his guests in a lordly fashion. The pigeons had returned with two black giant squirrels and several cackling hornbills. At a respectful distance, harvesting the back of the tree, were another two orang-utans, a mother and small infant. The youngster was getting plenty of experience at fending for himself for he was quite unable to keep up with the speed at which his mother moved about selecting choice titbits. The twittering and wing-clapping of the doves attracted more of their friends and a trio of hooting gibbons leaped across the wide gap to join the throng. Using branches as springboards they rocked up and down before launching themselves into the air. The gibbons worked swiftly, plucking off the red figs and popping them into mouths that were already full. Deserting his elders, a young gibbon tried to persuade the infant orang to join in a game of poke and run, 'you can't catch me', but in spite of his equal size the baby was not up to such agility and scuttled back to his mother for protection. After a quick circuit of the whole tree the gibbons moved on again, leaping away on their rounds.

Another female orang-utan arrived with her juvenile and clambered up the fig-root ladder. The first mother decided that the place was becoming too popular for comfort and prepared to leave. Arm over arm she cautiously descended the liana, looking all around to check that it was safe. With complete disrespect for his mother's careful precautions the baby came tumbling after her and clinging to the thin root slid down in one swift descent like a practised fireman.

As the day warmed up the doves and hornbills flew off and the other animals gradually dispersed till Redbeard was left in sole possession. He had moved his bed and was reclining in another of his four nests. During the afternoon more visitors arrived for a meal and he was soon entertaining a female orang-utan and her two young and a host of clattering hornbills. An adolescent male orang began to heave himself up the narrow rope but Redbeard uttered a string of deep bubbles warning the newcomer to keep clear. Not daring to disobey, the poor youngster had to search elsewhere for something to eat. With evening the crowd thinned and the mother and baby returned for a quick supper.

A marbled cat (left) snarls in alarm, hunched over in the characteristic bent-backed defensive posture that the delicate felines instinctively assume when they are standing or sitting. On the move, however, their slender bodies are extended in typical cat fashion. An arboreal animal, the marbled cat often comes to the ground to pursue rodents.

A Sumatran tiger (right) relaxes in the shade of a tree. Although the big cats can usually tolerate extremes in temperature, the torrid afternoon sun seems to cause tigers great discomfort. Unlike most cats, they love the water and bathe frequently—partly to escape the heat.

Insular Miniatures

A scientific theory holds that as certain species of animals traveled from their original mainland habitats to new island environments, they became smaller and darker as they moved farther away from the continent. The miniaturization process is strikingly demonstrated by the three Indonesian subspecies of tigers, the Sumatran (above), the Javan and the Balinese, all relations of the Bengal tiger of India. From the westernmost Sumatran tiger to the Balinese at the eastern extreme, all these subspecies are progressively smaller than their majestic mainland forebear and all have stripes that are set more closely together, giving them a darker overall appearance. (The Bengal tiger itself is smaller and darker than its nearest northerly cousin, the Siberian tiger.)

According to the same theory, the Indonesian marbled cat (opposite) is widely considered to be a slightly smaller replica of the Asian clouded leopard, and is found on the continent and on Formosa, Sumatra, Java and Borneo. Proof of the theory is elusive in this case, since the clouded leopard itself also inhabits Sumatra and Borneo.

A flying lizard at rest (left) seems to be no more than an extension of the branch on which it is perched. In flight, however, its skin flaps unfurl to reveal colors as dazzling as those of the most flamboyant butterflies.

A female colugo hangs upside down from a limb by her claws in order to cradle her infant snugly within her folded membranes (top, right). Most colugos spend the day dangling vertically by their front feet, becoming active at dusk when they begin to feed on fruits, buds, leaves and flowers.

Silhouetted against the twilight sky, an airborne colugo (right) shows off its gliding membranes. Colugos are as skillful at climbing as they are at gliding. On the ground, however, they are virtually helpless.

Air Time

To survive among the tall trees of the Indonesian rain forest, a few animals have adopted ways of taking to the air to get from one tree to another, rather than living on the ground and risking the dangers that lurk there. Among these aerialists are the so-called flying lizard (opposite) and the flying lemur (above and left). Neither creature actually flies, but rather glides on membranes that may be extended kitelike on either side of its body. The flying lizard, a member of the genus *Draco*, supports its membranes on five or six pairs of ribs that unfold in flight like a fan, stretching the skin taut. In this way the lizard can soar distances of over 50 feet.

The flying lemur, more accurately called the colugo, does not fly and is in no way related to the lemurs. It is in an order of its own and is perhaps the most efficient arboreal glider. The colugo's skin flaps are so extensive that it can drift through the air over a distance of more than 85 feet.

Mudskippers

When the muddy surface of an Indonesian tidal flat or estuary seems to be alive with movement, the cause is often the activity of mudskippers—six-inch-long fish that swim underwater, walk across the mud flats or even climb trees with equal aplomb. It may have been the warm sun or potential food supply among the exposed mangrove roots, and the juicy insects and crustaceans in the rich mud at the forest's edge, that first tempted the tiny fish to take up their amphibious ways.

Whatever the reason, mudskippers are well adapted for the double life. Pectoral fins are used both for balance in the water and as limbs for skipping about on the muddy banks. The mudskipper can bound as high as eight inches— apparently a territorial display—by violent contractions and expansions of its body. The mudskipper's eyes, atop its head, project eerily like miniature periscopes from the dark water as the little creature swims just under the surface. Underwater, a mudskipper breathes through gills, and on land it mixes air with water held in its gill chambers. The membranes lining the back of its mouth and throat are richly supplied with blood vessels, and through these membranes the animal gains an additional oxygen supply.

Two mudskippers confront each other aggressively (left). Such confrontations are not matters of life and death: Suddenly one animal will lunge, knocking the other over, but then it will skip hurriedly away.

Tails dipped nonchalantly in the water to maintain skin moisture, mudskippers bask in the sun (left). The pectoral fins, like chubby arms, raise the creature's torso out of the water.

A party of mudskippers ascends a tree—a feat that members of this species, shown at right, manage through an adaptation of their pelvic fins, which form a functional suction mechanism. Mudskippers climb trees, possibly to obtain food or perhaps to supplement their intake of oxygen, which is sometimes in short supply in the muddy water.

New Zealand

In lonely isolation in the southern reaches of the South Pacific, over 1,200 miles east-southeast of Australia and 1,600 miles north of Antarctica, New Zealand has probably never been connected with any continent by land bridges. Like so many other islands, New Zealand was formed 60 million years ago by movement of the earth's great plates. As the Pacific plate began to dive beneath the Australian plate along the 30,000-foot-deep Kermadec and Tonga trenches, the buckling rocks surfaced in the ocean as two main islands and a sprinkling of satellites on the westward side of the trenches. As a consequence of its isolation, virtually all of New Zealand's wildlife has had to come to it from across the sea, drifting with the ocean currents or borne on the winds.

Animals surviving the long ocean passage found islands larger in area but cooler in climate than either Hawaii or the Galápagos. New Zealand consists of two main islands, North Island and South Island, separated by the 16-mile Cook Strait, plus a host of tiny islets, with a combined area of 103,736 square miles (about the size of Colorado). The islands span about 900 miles from north to south. Coastal New Zealand has a cool, temperate climate, with few extremes of heat or cold.

Rainfall is high: North Island gets an overall 52 inches a year, while some parts of South Island are inundated with more than 200 inches, and others are left high and dry with less than 15 inches. North Island is hilly, with high plateaus and smoking volcanoes rising to 9,000 feet. South Island is more rugged, with deep fjords, mighty glaciers and loftier snow-capped mountains—the highest peak in the southern alps, Mount Cook, is over 12,000 feet and there are 17 peaks over 10,000 feet. When European settlers first arrived in the mid-19th century, the islands were largely covered with evergreen forest. Today much of the country has been cleared and is now grazing land.

Like other remote oceanic islands, New Zealand has a strongly unbalanced vertebrate animal population, with a high percentage of endemic species. The only mammal that ever reached New Zealand on its own was the peripatetic bat. New Zealand has two species, the wattled bat from Australia and an endemic short-tailed bat. All the deer, sheep, weasels, hedgehogs, opossums and rabbits now in New Zealand have been imported by man.

Of amphibians and reptiles, New Zealand acquired only a scattering—but they include some real zoological anach-ronisms. The only amphibians are three species of a single endemic genus of tiny frogs, *Leiopelma*, the most archaic of living frogs. New Zealand's reptiles number about 30: 17 small geckos (three endemic genera) and 13 skinks, along with one of the most venerable zoological antiques anywhere, an ancient lizardlike creature called the tuatara, which is perhaps the world's champion "living fossil." There are only four orders comprising the living reptiles: the chelonians (turtles and tortoises), the squamata (lizards and snakes), the crocodilia (crocodiles), and the rhynchocephalians ("beakheads"). The first three orders are widespread, but the fourth, the rhynchocephalians, has been reduced to a single living species, the tuatara, which lives only in New Zealand.

Outwardly, the tuatara resembles a lizard, two feet or more in length, with a crest of spines along its neck and back. Inwardly, however, its bone structure reveals its primitive nature: It has a stronger skull than lizards, buttressed internally by bone arches, unusual concave vertebrae and hooklike processes on its ribs, and a vestigial third eye on the top of its head, which reacts to heat. The tuatara is the last remnant of an order that flourished on the continents during the Age of the Dinosaurs, 200 million years ago, but died out everywhere except in New Zealand.

The glories of New Zealand's native wildlife are its birds. New Zealand has 308 species. One endemic parrot, the green kea (opposite), has become predatory. In the short time since Europeans introduced sheep to the islands, the carrion-eating kea somehow acquired a taste for sheep fat. It has learned to swoop down on the flocks, slashing at their backs to get at their fat.

In its predator-free remoteness, New Zealand has nurtured the largest collection of flightless birds of any island anywhere—all, naturalists believe, descended from birds that originally arrived on the islands on the wing and became grounded when the need for flight disappeared. The largest of these was the now-extinct, ostrichlike giant moa, which stood 12 feet tall and was completely wingless. There are two living flightless members of the rail family: the brownish-black wekas, and the takahe, a large indigo-blue bird with red beak and feet, which was long thought to be extinct until it was rediscovered by an ornithologist in 1948. Most notable is the ungainly kiwi (so called in imitation of its call), which so captivates New Zealanders that they have made it their national bird. The kiwi has

rudimentary wings so small they cannot be seen and—alone among birds—a long slender beak with facial bristles and sensitive nostrils at its tip for sniffing out worms, grubs and insects in the soft ground. One of the most poignant of all bird stories is that of New Zealand's flightless wren. In 1894, a cat belonging to the lighthouse keeper on Stephens Island in Cook Strait brought in 11 dead specimens of a hitherto unknown species of wren, which scientists named *Traversia lyalli* or the Stephens Island wren. Subsequently the cat captured a few more individuals—and then no more. "The history of this species, so far as human contact is concerned, begins and ends with the exploits of a domestic cat," ornithologist W.R.B. Oliver has noted. "The cat which discovered the species also immediately exterminated it."

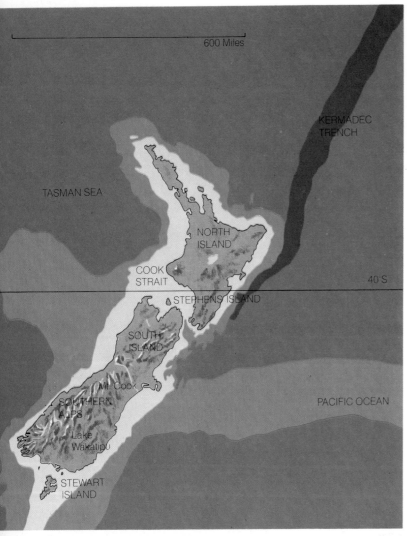

Tropical growth confronts snowcapped mountains across Lake Wakatipu on New Zealand's South Island. This varied environment favors animals, but the region's isolation prevented more than a few species from ever arriving to take advantage of it.

Grounded

Flightless birds were once commonplace on islands where, unthreatened by carnivorous predators, they lost the need for flight. New Zealand, a roomy island habitat, has been the home of many of the odd birds, including the moas, one of which, at 12 feet high, was the tallest bird that ever lived. Now extinct, it was until fairly recent times a bizarre sight sprinting across New Zealand grasslands, its shaggy feathers blowing about and crest waving, on large, ungainly-looking feet. *Dinornis*, its generic designation, means "terrible bird," but actually the moa was a peace-loving creature. The birds now live on only in Maori folklore.

The plump, sturdy little kiwi (overleaf) belongs to the same order of running birds as the moa and is the moa's present-day relative. But the kiwi has evolved a long, slightly curving bill with nostrils near the tip—an indis-

pensable tool in foraging for earthworms in the scrub belts above the tree line. It is nocturnal and compensates for weak eyesight by groping along, feeling its way carefully with tactile bristles distributed around its bill. The takahe (right) is the size of a duck and is now so close to extinction that only about 200 to 300 remain in existence. The omnivorous weka (below) is curious and impertinent, but its charm is not at all apparent to chicken farmers whose eggs are eaten by the fearless little creature. The kakapo (overleaf) is a flightless parrot with a slightly hooked bill. It has wings but has only a vestigial keel bone, and the flight muscles that are attached to the bone are weak, making sustained flight impossible. The Auckland Island duck (overleaf) is also unable to fly, though it can flutter 15 or 20 feet up a cliffside to reach its nest.

The weka (left), a strong, flightless rail, is regarded as beneficial because it eats insect pests and weasels, as well as mice and rats—keeping New Zealand's rodent population under control. It is also considered something of a nuisance because of its habit of invading campsites and pilfering shiny objects.

A resilient beak enables the takahe (above) to strip snowgrass stalks of leaves and eat only the base, which makes up its staple diet. The takahe nests in the upland regions, 2,900 feet or more above sea level, making a small, cozy bower with a thick grass lining to insulate it against inclement weather.

The kakapo (opposite) has a parrot's hooked beak and colorful plumage, with feathers surrounding its face, like an owl. Kakapos nest in an unlikely spot for a bird, burrowing under the root of a tree.

The coloration of the Auckland Island flightless duck (right) blends in with the kelp beds near its seaside nests. On foot, it sometimes ventures inland to feed at freshwater streams.

A kiwi (right) prepares for a meal by assuming a "tripod" position—feet planted firmly, bill extended close to the ground. Its sensitive nostrils can pick up the scent of insects or grubs, which it rapidly unearths with its long, efficient bill.

The spiny, dragonlike dorsal crest of the animal at left inspired its name, tuatara, a Maori word meaning "spine bearer." Tuataras are slow-growing creatures with a remarkable longevity—up to 70 years.

The leiopelma (below) is one of the three species of frog endemic to New Zealand. It is regarded as a scientific wonder because amphibians are rarely found in remote island habitats. The mystery deepens in the absence of evidence that it ever existed outside of New Zealand.

Anomalous Elders

The tuatara (opposite) is the only living representative of an order of reptiles that roamed the continents during the Age of Dinosaurs. This primitive reptile and an ancient amphibian, the leiopelma frog (above), thrived in the cool, moist New Zealand climate for tens of thousands of years, free from predators.

The tuatara, a solitary creature that emits a testy hiss if disturbed, has survived unchanged for 100 million years. Although the rats, mice and other mammals introduced by 19th century Europeans destroyed the populations on the main New Zealand islands, the rugged reptilians hold their own on about 30 small, offshore islets. Always threatened by island-hopping rats, though, the tuatara remains endangered, and Stephens Island, one of its last strongholds, has been designated as a reserve. The prehistoric holdover lives on there, free from predators, digging burrows in the loose soil or taking refuge in nesting holes that have been abandoned by shearwaters.

113

Japan

The Japanese archipelago is one of four island arcs stretching more than 2,300 miles from the Kuril Islands to Taiwan. These islands began to rise out of the Pacific Ocean 40 to 50 million years ago, heaved up by the colossal forces of a collision between the earth's great crustal plates—an earth-shifting process that continues in a northwesterly direction at the rate of several inches a year. As the huge Pacific plate inches northwestward, its leading edge collides with the plate forming the Asian continent and slides underneath, forming as it does so a series of trenches which are the ocean's deepest abysses. As the plate descends, it also forces up the massive mountains and steaming volcanoes of the Japanese home islands.

The Japanese archipelago, then, is of oceanic origin, with its foundations resting on the continental shelf of Asia. At times, however, there was a closer link with the mainland. During the Ice Ages, when worldwide sea levels were lower than they are today, the Japanese islands were connected to one another and to the Eurasian continent by land bridges, both in the southwest, across the shallow 125-mile-wide Korea Strait, and in the north, from the island of Sakhalin across the Tatar Strait. These Eurasian connections enabled animals to move back and forth and endowed the islands with a large and varied animal population.

Japan proper offers animals a sizable area (142,774 square miles) on its four major islands—Hokkaido in the north, Honshu, the main island, and Shikoku and Kyushu in the south—and a temperate climate comparable to that of the eastern United States from Maine to Florida.

Hokkaido, like Maine, is covered with conifers mixed with deciduous forests; the southern Japanese islands are warmed by the Kuroshio Current just as the southeastern United States is warmed by the Gulf Stream, and have palms and other subtropical vegetation. Overall rainfall is ample, 40 to 60 inches a year. Like the eastern United States, Japan is also the scene of the recurrent drama of four marked seasons, the cherry blossoms of spring and verdure of summer followed by the flaming foliage of autumn and heavy snows of winter. A large difference between the two regions, however, is the fact that Japan is far more mountainous than the eastern United States: Fujiyama rises over 12,000 feet, and the Japan Alps in central Honshu have many peaks of more than 10,000 feet. Over 80 percent of the country is covered with mountains.

With such a favorable environment, the Japanese islands support a rich selection of wildlife, a well-balanced, harmonic fauna. Its streams abound with freshwater fish and numerous amphibians, including the world's largest, the Japanese giant salamander, which grows up to five feet in length and is now a rigidly protected species and has been declared, in quaintly Japanese style, a "national monument." As the habitat of hundreds of species of land birds, Japan is an ornithologist's paradise.

The dainty little sika deer, the endangered shaggy goat-antelope, or serow, which has been reduced in numbers to 3,000 to 5,000 individuals, and the raccoon dog, a nocturnal creature with a bandit mask around its eyes, are among the other creatures that are typically Japanese.

The most engaging of all Japanese mammals are perhaps the Japanese macaque monkeys, or "snow monkeys," an endemic species and the monkey with the northernmost habitat in the world. True to their nickname, these monkeys have become so well adapted to northern winters that they seem to enjoy playing in the snow.

Beyond the Japanese home islands, the extended archipelago stretches over four distinct faunal zones, from glacial palaearctic in the north to subtropical in the south, and a gamut of extreme weather conditions. The two dozen Kuril Islands in the north formed an arm of the Bering Strait land bridge between Asia and North America during the Ice Ages, and their animals are largely hardy species that are common to both the Old and the New Worlds—brown bears, sea otters, walruses and seals. Sakhalin, a sizable, forested island 589 miles long, is also a wintry place, the home of wintry wildlife—bears, wolves, wolverines, sables, reindeer and the great Siberian tiger. Temperatures in Sakhalin average −10° F. in midwinter, and the five-mile-wide Tatar Strait freezes over, providing a bridge of sorts to the Siberian mainland.

South of Japan proper, the Ryukyu Islands are scattered like stepping-stones along the East China Sea from Kyushu to Taiwan, and temperatures are milder and more temperate than those in the north of the archipelago. Of the more than 80 species of terrestrial animals in the entire island chain at least two are unique, both of them on the verge of extinction and both from the Ryukyus. The Iriomote cat, a medium-sized felid which was discovered only in the mid-1960s and which numbers no more than 150 individuals, inhabits just one tiny island south of Okinawa. The Ryukyu hare, a curious, short-eared, short-legged insular

rabbit that is a relict relative of a race of long-extinct prehistoric rabbits, survives only on two isolated islands in the northern Ryukyus. Both animals are protected and, in the case of the hare, the Japanese government has decreed that "it is also strictly prohibited to capture the species without special permission" and asserts that "it is forbidden by the game law, it will never become extinct."

Taiwan (formerly Formosa), the southern anchor of the island chain, has a large population of native animals which are all quite similar to Chinese forms on the mainland, 100 miles across the Formosa Strait. The island is the home of several rapidly disappearing species, including the yellow-throated marten and the clouded leopard, both creatures of the diminished forests of Taiwan, and the rare Taiwanese black bear, also known as the moon bear, identifiable by the distinctive Y-shaped mark on its chest which islanders have likened to the shape of a bird of prey. Taiwan almost certainly got its oriental fauna by way of the relatively shallow Formosa Strait, which, during the Ice Ages, was a land bridge to the coast of China.

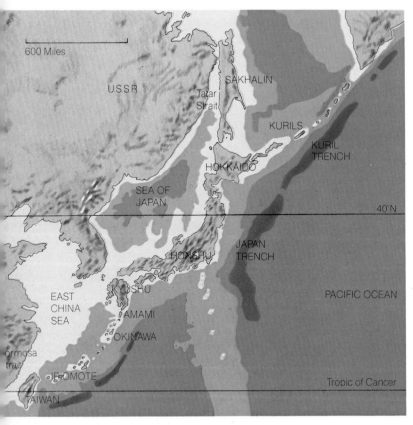

Waters of a hot spring high in the mountains of Kyushu, Japan, glow beneath a pine. Japan's mountains—taking up 80 per cent of its territory—help ensure the survival of wildlife in islands that are among the most densely populated regions in the world.

Legends of Nippon

Japan is home, on a full- or part-time basis, to some of the world's largest and most stately birds, including the long-necked species on these pages.

The Japanese crane (below), with a bill-to-tail length of 53 inches, is the largest crane in Japan. This long-legged creature is found in Manchuria, Korea and northern Japan. Like all members of its family, the Japanese crane is known for its exuberant dancing, which takes place all year long but especially during courtship. Both sexes join in the lively jumping, and even immature birds are active participants. Cranes are symbols of longevity to the Japanese: According to their folklore, the birds are supposed to live 1,000 years. The oldest known crane fell far short of the legendary mark, living to be only 43 years old in captivity.

The Japanese white stork (opposite, below) is another symbol of long life in Japan. The actual future of the big birds is a sad refutation of the myth, however, for they are seriously endangered in Japan, with a population of only 15 storks reported in 1966.

The regal whooper swan (opposite, above) is a snow-white bird that frequents the higher latitudes of the Northern Hemisphere. Whoopers migrate widely, and after nesting in the tundras of Eurasia they move southward, wintering in China, Japan and throughout northern Europe.

Three whooper swans splash playfully (above) in a Japanese lake. These large, graceful birds are legally protected in their regular visiting places. Whoopers are sociable birds that create a formidable din when they gather in large flocks. On the water they carry their long necks in a characteristic stiff pose. In flight their necks are extended.

Snow up to their ankles does not dampen the spirits of a group of Japanese cranes (left). Inhabitants of marshlands, wet plains and moors, they feed on the move alone or in family groups. Japanese cranes are graceful fliers that need a running start before they take off. In the air the flock flies in either a line or V formation.

Two young Japanese white storks wait in their large twig and grass nest in a pine tree (right) while their parents forage for food. At first the hatchlings are fed on partially digested food from both their parents. Later worms, frogs, fish, insects, birds and even small mammals make up their diet.

A handsome raccoon dog (left) treks alertly through the thick underbrush in search of food. Although they are now being bred successfully in captivity, wild raccoon dogs are quite rare in Japan, where they are hunted not only for their fur and flesh but also for their bones, which are used for medicinal purposes.

Two Japanese serows (opposite) rouse at the sound of an approaching intruder from their sheltered resting place in the snow. Under pressure serows can effectively defend themselves with their slightly curved horns, which may grow as long as 10 inches.

Mammal Potpourri

Among the 80 species of land mammals found in Japan, two are extraordinary patchworks of mammalian attributes. The raccoon dog (left) has its coon namesake's masklike facial markings and long-haired coat; otherwise it more nearly resembles a fox. Raccoon dogs are primarily nocturnal omnivores whose diet consists of small rodents and fish as well as acorns and seasonal berries and fruits. They live solitarily or in small family groups that take up residence either in burrows deserted by other animals or in dens they construct themselves in rocky crevices and thickets. Raccoon dogs inhabit Siberia, Manchuria, Korea and China as well as Japan. In the more northerly parts of their range they sometimes spend the worst part of the winter in a hibernationlike sleep, a characteristic that is unique among canids.

The Japanese serow (opposite), which also occurs on the island of Taiwan, is a horned, hoofed bovine commonly referred to as a goat antelope. Although they are bigger bodied, broader hoofed, slower and more heavy-footed than their swift and graceful antelope relatives, serows are nonetheless confident mountaineers in the manner of their close relatives, North American mountain goats. Serows negotiate the rugged, rocky cliffs of their island homes singly or in family groups of as many as six animals. They can live at altitudes of more than 8,000 feet, but when snow falls they descend to lower elevations in order to find the grass and leaves they feed on.

Celebrations of Nature

Haiku, the briefest and most popular form of Japanese poetry, is no more than a flash of words expressing a single conception in an instant. Although the subjects of haiku may be as diverse as a scarecrow's hat or a telegraph pole, the message is principally a seasonal salute to nature, and especially to animals and plants. The structure and meter of proper Japanese verse is traditionally and rigidly governed by rules that are more restrictive than the form of an English sonnet: Haiku may be no longer than 17 syllables, expressed in English translation in three unrhymed lines and in Japanese characters by a single vertical line.

Japanese art is also honored for its brevity: an idea conveyed in a single brush stroke. Not surprisingly, haiku and art often complement each other. On these pages is a poem by Issa (1762–1827), one of the most celebrated of the haiku poets, and one by Hekigotō (1873–1937), a more recent master, along with two paintings by Hokusai (1760–1849), the best known of Japanese artists, who died at 89, "an old man mad with painting."

Three wild geese
     Parents and child
          Return

               Issa

     Early spring
          Wading through the water
               A heron

               Hekigotō

123

Shaggy Monkeys

The monkey with the most northerly range in the world is the Japanese macaque. Relatives of the familiar rhesus monkeys of India, Japanese macaques have figured prominently·in the art, religion and folklore of Japan. It is three Japanese macaques that illustrate the familiar Buddhist maxim: "See no evil, hear no evil, speak no evil."

Japanese macaques (above)—unlike their relatives elsewhere—have long whiskers and beards, bare red faces and very dense, shaggy coats that protect them from heavy snow and temperatures that may dip as low as 20° F. They associate in organized groups, like the one at right, that usually number between 30 and 150 members. There is a definite hierarchy within the group, which is led by one or more young males acting as guides and guards for the rest. A separate rank order governs the females.

Today, Japanese macaques are legally protected in Japan, not because they are endangered but because they are playing a starring role in experiments by a group of Japanese scientists who believe that the social interactions of these animals can provide clues to human development.

Credits

Cover—S. Summerhays, Photo Researchers, Inc. 1—Oxford Scientific Films. 5—R. Kinne, P.R., Inc. 6—(left) Wolfgang Bayer, (right) Candice Bayer. 7—Z. Leszczynski, Animals Animals. 17–20—R. Kinne. P.R., Inc. 21—N. Myers, Bruce Coleman, Inc. 22—M. Austerman, Animals Animals. 22–23—R. Kinne, P.R., Inc. 24—Thase Daniel. 25–27—(top) R. Kinne, P.R., Inc. 27—(bottom) 30—N. Myers, B.C., Inc. 30–31—L. Dean, Time Inc. 32–33—F. Goro, Time Inc. 34–35—K. Fink, B.C., Inc. 35–36—(top) R. Kinne, P.R., Inc., (bottom) H. Uible, P.R., Inc. 37—R. Kinne, P.R., Inc. 39—R. Hernandez, P.R., Inc. 40–41—Sven Lindblad, P.R., Inc. 42—M. Castro, P.R., Inc. 43—D. Houston, B.C., Ltd. 44—(top) G. Holton, P.R., Inc. 44–45—M. Castro, P.R., Inc. 46—B. Coleman, B.C., Inc. 47—D. Houston, B.C., Ltd. 49—J. Carmichael, B.C., Inc. 50–51—C. Frank, P.R., Inc. 52—(top) J. Carmichael, B.C., Inc., (bottom) E. Bernard, B.C., Inc. 53—(top) J. Carmichael, P.R., Inc. 52–53—(bottom) R. Mendez, Animals Animals. 54—(top) R. Mendez, Animals Animals, (bottom) Oxford Scientific Films. 55—Thase Daniel. 56—J & D. Bartlett, B.C., Inc. 57—Oxford Scientific Films. 58—R. Mendez, Animals Animals. 59—(top) F. Erize, B.C., Inc. 59—(bottom) G. Clough B.C., Inc. 61—William Mull. 62–63—D. Budnik, Woodfin Camp. 64–65—Willaim Mull. 66—(top) P. Banko, (center and bottom) R. Western. 67—R. Western. 68—Candice Bayer. 69—R. Shallenberger, Ahuimanu Productions. 71—G. Harrison, B.C., Inc. 72–73—C. Anderson, Sea Library. 74–75—K. Tanaka, Animals Animals. 74—D. Cavagnaro. 75—T. DeRoy, B.C., Inc. 76—(top) N. Devore, III, B.C., Inc., (bottom) F. Erize, B.C., Inc. 77—(top) J. Running, Sea Library, (bottom) M. & B. Reed, Animals Animals. 78–79—T. DeRoy, B.C., Inc. 79—M. & B. Reed, Animals Animals. 82–83—N. Devore III, B.C., Inc. 83—(top) Peter B. Kaplan P.R., Inc. (bottom) T. DeRoy, B.C., Inc. 84–85—J. & D. Bartlett, B.C., Inc. 87—L. Burrows, Time Inc. 88–89—Co Rentmeester. 90–91—L. Burrows, Time Inc. 92—(top) Co Rentmeester, 92–93—I. Polunin. 93—Wolfgang Bayer. 98—D. & R. Sullivan, B.C., Inc., 99—Co Rentmeester. 100—C. Frith, B.C., Inc. 101—(top) P. Ward, B.C., Inc., (bottom) I. Polunin. 102–103—I. Polunin. 105—G. Schaller, B.C., Inc. 106–107—W. Ruth, B.C., Inc. 108—M. Soper, B.C., Inc. 109—I. MacPhail, B.C., Ltd. 110–113—M. Soper, B.C., Inc. 113—B. Enting, P.R., Inc. 115—K. Tanaka, Animals Animals. 116–117—G. Holton, P.R., Inc. 118—Nature Productions, P.R., 119–120—K. Tanaka, Animals Animals. 121—Nature Productions, P.R., Inc. 124—K. Tanaka, Animals Animals. 124–125—Nature Productions, P.R., Inc.

Photographs on endpapers are used courtesy of Time-Life Picture Agency, Russ Kinne and Stephen Dalton of Photo Researchers, Inc., and Nina Leen. Film sequence on page 8 is from "Green Ceiling of Borneo," a program in the Time-Life Television series *Wild, Wild World of Animals*.

MAPS by Nick Fasciano.

ILLUSTRATIONS pages 10 through 14 courtesy The N.Y. Public Library; those on pages 28–29 are by André Durenceau; the illustration on page 81 courtesy The N.Y. Public Library; those on pages 94–97 are by John Groth. The paintings on pages 122 and 123 are courtesy of the Smithsonian Institution, Freer Gallery of Art, Washington, D.C.

Bibliography

Allee, W. C. and Schmidt, Karl P., *Ecological Animal Geography*. John Wiley, 1951.

Allen, Robert Porter, *Birds of the Caribbean*. Viking, 1961

Anderson, Sydney and Jones, J. Knox Jr., *Recent Mammals of the World*. Ronald Press, 1967.

Beamish, Tony, *Aldabra Alone*. Sierra Club, 1970.

Beebe, William, *The Arcturus Adventure*. G.P. Putnam's Sons, 1926.

———. *Galápagos—World's End*. G. P. Putnam's Sons, 1924.

Bond, James, *Birds of the West Indies*. Houghton Mifflin, 1971.

Bowman, Robert I., *Morphological Differentiation and Adaptation in the Galápagos Finches*. University of California Press, 1961.

Calder, Nigel, *The Restless Earth*. Viking, 1962.

Carlquist, Sherwin, *Island Life*. The Natural History Press, 1965.

Carter, T. D., Hill, J. E. and Tate, G.H.H., *Mammals of the Pacific World*. The Macmillan Company, 1945.

Darlington, Philip J., *Zoogeography*. John Wiley, 1957.

Darwin, Charles, *The Voyage of the Beagle*. Doubleday, 1962.

Delacour, Jean and Mayr, Ernst, *Birds of the Philippines*. The Macmillan Company, 1946.

Eibl-Eibesfeldt, Irenaus, *Galápagos: The Noah's Ark of the Pacific*. Doubleday, 1961.

George, Wilma, *Animal Geography*. Heinemann, 1962.

Gosline, William A. and Brock, Vernon E., *Hawaiian Fishes*. University of Hawaii Press, 1960.

Harper, Francis, *Extinct and Vanishing Mammals of the Old World*. American Committee for International Wildlife Protection, 1945.

Heezen, Bruce C. and Hollister, Charles D., *The Face of the Deep*. Oxford University Press, 1971.

Heseltine, Nigel, *Madagascar*. Praeger, 1971.

Kay, E. Alison, ed., *A Natural History of the Hawaiian Islands*. University of Hawaii Press, 1972.

Mayr, Ernst, *Birds of the Southwest Pacific*. The Macmillan Company, 1945.

Matthews, Harrison, et al., *Fascinating World of Animals*. Reader's Digest Association, 1971.

Morris, Desmond, *The Mammals*. Harper and Row, 1965.

Munro, George C., *Birds of Hawaii*. Ridgeway Press, 1960.

Oliver, W.R.B., *New Zealand Birds*. A.H. and A.W. Reed, 1955.

Stoddart, D. R., "Retrospect and Prospect of Aldabra Research," *Nature*, March 15, 1969, pp. 1004–1006.

——— and Wright, C. A., "Ecology of Aldabra Atoll," *Nature*, March 25, 1967, pp. 1174–1117.

Sullivan, Walter, *Continents in Motion*. McGraw-Hill, 1974.

Walker, Ernest P., *Mammals of the World*. Johns Hopkins University Press, 1975.

Wallace, Alfred Russel, *Island Life*. The Macmillan Company, 1880.

———, *The Malay Archipelago*. Dover Publications, 1962.

Yamashina, Yoshimaro, *Birds in Japan*. Tokyo News Service, 1961.

Index